D0195107

NEXT YEAR COUNTRY

by

LORNEY FABER

ACKNOWLEDGEMENTS

To John and the kids for their patience and encouragement
To Mom for her faith in me
To my brother-in-law, Jim Faber, for the pictures
To Eldon Halingstad whose help made this book possible
To Sister M. Giswalda, O.S.F. and the others at St. Paul's mission for their prayers

Copyright © 1975 by Lorney Faber
All rights reserved

Printed and bound in the United States of America

published by
FORUM PUBLISHING COMPANY
888 Logan Street
Denver, Colorado 80203

Contents

TO MY MOTHER

Marion Kearful Vercruyssen

A true pioneer lady who gave so much of herself
to help so many others

Foreword

This is a true account of country living on a Montana ranch, written for those who love the outdoors and the wonders of nature.

For many, I hope, it will prove to be informative, as much of our knowledge of country things and the lore of our earlier settlers is being obscured by the relentless march of civilization. It needs to be recorded for posterity as a memorial to those who carved homesteads out of the bleak, unyielding prairies and the domineering mountains.

My roots go deep into the soil, for my grandfather came to Montana in 1888 on a work train. The railroad had made its first appearance into Montana only seven years earlier, some considerable distance to the south of Blaine County where he settled.

My grandfather, Jerry Kearful, purchased a team, wagon, some seed, and a few head of stock and proceeded to stake his claim. By dint of his hard labors, privations and sheer bull-headedness, he managed to build a good ranch and a good life.

This is only one isolated example of an early Montana man who stuck it out through the droughts, hail, range fires, grasshoppers, thieves and the depression. Many failed or just gave up. And still today, here and there, an empty grass-grown cellar hole, a broken crock and a few rotting logs give mute witness to what was once a man's fervent dream.

Most of these old timers have passed on now, but their children and grandchildren are carrying on in their stead. Some have gone away, only to return with master's degrees and a longing to go back to the land. The land calls to us for we belong to it. We are truly the stewards of the land – caring for it even better than we care for ourselves, so that it will remain to sustain the generations that follow us.

Times are different now than in my grandfather's day, but the people are the same and the life is never dull. From day to day it changes, always filled with excitement, satisfaction, bone weariness, and even danger as we try to work with nature in earning a living. We always hope and pray for next year to be a better one, but we take it all as it comes. We'll never be rich in money, but we're rich in other ways, and we leave a valuable heritage to our children.

I earnestly hope this book will help many to understand more fully what a strong force and what a staunch ally this great nation has in its western stockgrowers.

Lorney Faber

Chinook, Montana
March, 1975

1

Trails and Tales

"He that tilleth his land shall be satisfied with bread. . ."
Proverbs 12:11

Up ahead of me, the red dome light on the deputy sheriff's vehicle pierced the grey day with its intermittent warning to the oncoming traffic, as I crept slowly along the icy highway with my load of baled hay. Behind me, strung out along a two mile stretch, was our herd of cattle headed home to the winter ground. And behind them, and throughout them, were all the riders, sitting hunched up, a little askew, to get what protection they could from the biting chill wind that knifed through their clothing until their numbness forced them to get off their horses to stamp some life back into deadened feet and hands. Behind the last riders came another car representing the "law" with flashing red light.

The barrow pits were deep with snowdrifts so that we had little trouble keeping the cattle on the highway, for it was the only place where they could walk. The heat from the sickly sun over the past few days had melted some of the ice on the asphalt. All of the coulees were blown full of the slightly crusted snow, making it impossible for us to trail across country; and all of the back roads were a frozen glare of ice that made it dangerous for a brood cow, heavy with calf, to walk there. The only way home was straight up the busy highway, so that is just where we were, with the traffic even heavier than usual because of the approaching holiday season.

A semi with an extra long trailer snaked up alongside of me with its emergency flashers on. The driver gave me a friendly wave and went on around a car that had parked to let him go by. I relaxed a bit. Maybe this was going to work out okay after all. We had only eight miles to go until we could leave the highway, and so far it had gone without a hitch. At first the cattle, not knowing my voice, would not come when I called them. I continued calling them and at the same time kept throwing off a few flakes of alfalfa. They reluctantly began to follow either because I was so hoarse I was sounding like my husband, or they were so bewildered they'd follow anyone.

Just then a red sports car appeared on the scene. The driver was coming too fast for the road conditions and he ignored the deputy's lights and signaling arm. The car had only just passed me when a contrary old brindle cow started across the lane of traffic. The driver applied his brakes and slid sideways, burning rubber. He righted himself for an instant and then swapped ends on the ice and skidded some more. By this time he was beating a staccato blast on his horn.

I stopped the pickup and jumped out. Miraculously, the brindle cow, unscathed, was walking placidly up the wrong lane, stopping cars as she went. But behind me confusion ensued. About twenty head had found a railroad approach, had headed onto it, and were now high-tailing it back down the tracks in the direction from which they had come. Another ten or fifteen had jumped out into the barrow pit and were wallowing around in belly-deep snow, lunging and falling through the crust. I quickly cut the twine on another bale of hay and began throwing it out while I called the other cattle that had now hesitated on the highway. I was facing into the wind and before long my eyes were running, keeping me from seeing the commotion and flurry of activity farther down the road.

Meanwhile, the driver of the red car had maneuvered his way around, continuing on his way with poor grace. Just then I was far too busy coaxing the cows out of the ditch and back up onto the road to worry much about ill-tempered motorists. The deputy had pulled out into the middle of the highway to stop all traffic for a time.

By the time the cattle had worked themselves out of the ditch, bribed by the good hay I was throwing recklessly about, I spotted the others coming toward me up the train tracks. A cowboy on a steaming horse was hot on their trail. I sent a swift prayer Heavenward as I knew that not all of the riders had their horses shod and it was very treacherous going. Without the sharp calks on the horses' Never Slips (horseshoes) to insure their footing, a horse and rider could upend on the ice faster than you could bat an eyelash. Our own children were riding safe, old, reliable cow horses, but they were nevertheless "barefooted" and I had repeatedly warned the kids that morning to "hang loose."

About the time we had the cattle moving along again, and the traffic had begun its endless course through our procession, another dreaded peril reared its ugly head. A westbound passenger train was catching us fast. Now, I know that they must sound their horn at all crossings, but it did seem a little superfluous that day. Anyway, we were pretty busy for the next half hour gathering up cattle that had bolted in all directions at the sound of the train's long loud blast.

Weary eons later, when we were safely away from the noisy highway where we could rest the cattle and ourselves a bit, I slumped in the seat, soaking up the warmth from the heater and let my mind wander at will. The riders were warming up with thermos coffee and doughnuts, all slightly crumbled by our three-year-old son. He'd been raiding the lunch box all morning while I was too preoccupied to care whether or not he took a bite from each one.

My mind whirled like a kaleidoscope with flashing images of remembered scenes falling into place before me. This was no trail drive as in my grandfather's time, or even as I remembered as a little girl. This was trailing in the style of the 1970's where the whole family had turned out, helped by willing friends.

The kaleidoscope swept pictures across my closed eyelids. I was in the drug store of the local town looking for a particular kind of cookbook I liked. It was completely blank so you could write in whatever recipes you wanted. When I inquired, the clerk looked at me in real astonishment and asked, "But does anyone cook with recipes any more? I thought everyone used mixes. No, I'm sorry we don't have anything like that." I wanted to tell her a few things, but her beautifully coiffured head was turning away with a jingle of earrings, and her attention and perfume wafted elsewhere.

I wanted very much to tell her about a sumptuous feast I had once enjoyed that my mother had cooked entirely on nothing more than a potbellied heating stove. There is nothing to equal the flavor of potatoes baked in the ashes, and chocolate cake baked in an old black iron frying pan resting on the coals. I wanted her to know about the invigorating scent of pitch burning and snapping in a wood cookstove in the morning, mingled with the aroma of frying bacon, sourdough pancakes and freshly brewed coffee.

Sadly, I turned away. In her world of frozen waffles and precooked omelets, she would never know these things; and I

might just as well go home and write down the recipes for my daughters in a plain ruled notebook.

Again, I was back in another store. This time I was waiting in line to buy white material to make a First Communion dress for our second daughter. I was paying no attention to the two young ladies ahead of me, as I was hoping to get home in time to feed my forty-six orphan lambs their bottles without hurrying too much before time to start supper. I was speculating on whether there'd be enough spuds in the house or if I'd have to go to the cellar for more.

Suddenly, something one of them said caught my attention and I began to listen. Clearly, one said to the other, "Why, I can remember when my mother had to do all the washing in an old Maytag and then hang it all out on the clothesline!"

At that point, I stopped listening and went back over the years until I could picture my own mother bent over a wash tub and scrubbing board out by the back door. She was humming "Cowboy Jack," the only song I had ever heard her sing in my life, and she put a lot of effort into each garment as she rubbed it over the board. A meadowlark was singing nearby, and really, you could say that the prairie was blooming.

She hung our washing on the sagebrush to dry in the sun; and what a delicious smell it imparted to our clothes. Maybe that is why I still like the smell of the sage. But if you don't believe me when I say that the prairie was in bloom, then you've never seen a checkered tablecloth draped over a tall sagebush, with three pairs of pink cotton underpants adorning another bush nearby!

The pictures turned again and fell into focus. This time I was waiting in line in a supermarket forty miles away to buy candy bars and bananas to tide the little ones over until we got home and made supper. Two men in front of me were talking.

One asked the other, "How have you been getting along?"

The second one replied, "Oh, I guess the same as always. I work all week for my pay so I can come down here and give it all to the farmers!"

I looked closely at the second individual. He was of middle age and dressed casually in sports clothes. I glanced at his purchases in the push cart. They consisted of two packs of beer, two cartons of cigarettes, an aerosol can of something or other, two TV dinners, and a box of fancy crackers. I knew then that the farmers' message wasn't getting through to the public.

The kaleidoscope turned again and I was sitting in a comfortably furnished home visiting with a well-groomed, well-spoken friend who lived in that same city. As the dinner hour approached, she apologized for not asking me to stay, but excused herself by saying that all she had in the house was one can of tomato soup and only a little bread. She had not yet done the marketing for the day.

I wondered what her several children would eat when I left, and wanted to make the suggestion that she stir up a batch of hot biscuits, but was afraid to embarrass her in case she didn't keep flour and baking powder in the house. I've thought of her often, and worried some, for what if she was unable, for some reason, to get to the store every day and buy just what they needed to eat for that one day only. To me, it seemed a precarious way to live, considering the huge meals we serve three times a day at the ranch to any and all who happen to be there at mealtime.

My mental review was suddenly stopped when I heard my husband, John, hollering to get the cattle moving for home again. I started the pickup slowly up the road; but, since the cattle now knew where they were and wanted to get home just as badly as I did, they didn't require much watching, so my mind was free to ponder.

We're nothing more nor less than average ranch folks, running a family operation of the kind, I am told, that is fast disappearing, being swallowed up by large corporations. And yet, I know of many others just like us. Are we a vanishing breed? I don't know and sincerely hope not, for it's more than just a living to us, it's a way of life. Our kind does not own stock in munitions plants back east or winter homes in the south. Nor do we vacation all winter. We stay right here in the cold old north, feeding the livestock that helps put meat on America's tables.

But our kind does dream a lot. We dream of next year when the drought will break, next year when the calf and lamb crop will be better, next year when the new alfalfa seeding will really produce. Next year, maybe the livestock prices will be up so we can afford a new hay swather, and maybe the spring will be mild with no calf and lamb scours (diarrhea). Maybe it won't freeze up in August again, and maybe the coyotes won't kill so many of the lambs. We might even take a day or two off and call it a vacation. Our kind of rancher lives in a next year country.

We are the ones who mow around a duck nest in a hay field. We are the ones who are concerned about erosion and take steps to stop it. We need no agency to tell us what to do and how to do it. We're down here at the grass roots level, experiencing things first hand.

I've seen my husband shake his head when thirty-five deer camped overnight in our second cutting haystacks and raised havoc. The snow was terribly deep that winter, and hay was selling for seventy-five dollars a ton. Yet, he only shook his head, knowing the deer had to eat somewhere or perish, although he would have preferred that they go elsewhere.

We are the guardians of the land in this Big Sky Country and Land of Shining Mountains. Who will tell of our struggles, trials and perils? Who will tell our story, for there are so many of us?

I resolved then and there to try to put down on paper what it is like out here in "next year country," so that maybe our city brethren will understand us a little better.

2

Bunkhouse Baloney

"The life of a labourer that is content with what he hath, shall be sweet. . ."
Ecclesiasticus 40:18 (Douay)

It was one of those rare summer days that a person would like to recapture again. The wind was not blowing but neither were the mosquitos out. The sky was a clear blue, with only a few fluffy white clouds to lend an interesting pattern. It was early enough that the grass was a bright green and wildflowers dotted the coulees and hillsides with gay little spots of color here and there.

The curlews gave their plaintive cries, and on one of the big reservoirs, two pairs of Canadian geese escorted their flotilla of fluffy ducklings away from the shoreline into the comparative safety of deeper water.

A slight shower had delayed the haying for the morning, so we had all gone to the north range to capture a butcher beef. We had loaded two horses into the horse trailer. When we found the one we wanted, John would unload the horses and rope the beef. We would drag it into the trailer and haul it off to town. He had in mind a certain three-year-old that had lost her calf, but changed his mind when we arrived at the range.

Instead, he decided upon an ornery old steer that was out of an equally ornery old milk cow. It was impossible to keep that steer where he belonged. He could run and jump like a deer; and he had long murderous horns to boot. This particular day, John happened to know that the steer was in the neighbor's field, so we headed on over that way and unloaded our horses when we came upon a bunch of cattle with this mean steer in their midst.

The idea was that our second daughter, Jody, who was then only six, would ride the other horse; and when John had the critter roped, I would drive the pickup and trailer up close to load it. Great idea, but when the steer saw us, he took off like a shot across the prairie. John was right after him, but missed with his first loop.

They came to a fence. The steer, with his own peculiar brand of osmosis, went through it without a falter, but left John looking for a gate. Meanwhile, I was carefully driving my way along, on the lookout for boulders and cactus patches.

By the time I had passed through the gate and gone over a slight rise, I saw the two riders in a low basin chasing the steer around what looked like about a quarter-mile of old, fallen-down barbed wire fence. The steer could cross it at will, but the riders had to be more careful. I saw John's horse tangle up in some of the wire and come to an abrupt halt.

The next instant, I was out and running to head the steer off, leaving our oldest girl, Marion, to suffer the fate of all oldest daughters, that of watching the current baby in the pickup.

I hollered and flapped my arms wildly in a vain attempt to head the steer off, but onward he came. By now, he was on the fight and ready to take on anything that moved. The sight of my ludicrous dancing about only infuriated him further. He lowered his horns and came at me with a rush.

I can remember how dry my mouth became. There was no protection of any kind where I stood, not even a stick, only grass and cactus. Involuntarily, I stepped backward and my ankle turned under me. I fell heavily to the ground, and not a moment too soon to escape serious injury. I'll never forget how his flying hoofs and the dirty hair on his belly looked as he jumped over my sprawled body and continued on his flight to freedom.

Shakily, I got up and saw Jody riding toward me at a fast lope. Now, I am short and stocky; and regardless of all the long hours spent as a youngster in practicing fancy mounting, I never got to first base. A horse simply must stand still for me so I can grasp the saddle horn with one hand and turn the stirrup around with the other hand to mount.

But this day, I had my shining hour and no one was even there to witness it. I shall never be able to duplicate it. As Jody's horse galloped by, I grabbed the saddle horn and swung up behind her in a fashion that would have made even Roy Rogers envious. So maybe all that fancy stuff is only an overdose of adrenalin after all.

By this time, we saw that John had extricated himself from the wire and had roped the steer not too far away. The crazed animal was still on the warpath and was punishing John's horse cruelly with his horns at every opportunity, so I don't think John was sorry when he had to "dump" the critter a couple of times to cool him off. We got the animal loaded without much further trouble; and when we were all once again in the pickup headed to town, leaving our horses tied to a fence corner to await our return, I came in for much praise and open admiration from the kids.

I was embarrassed by their continued refrain, "Oh, Mom, you looked just like a bullfighter! Weren't you even scared?"

My conscience finally got the better of me and I had to tell them the truth, even though I hated to do so. It was so deflating to have to say in all reality that I had been scared "spitless" and that, really, I had clumsily fallen down instead of employing some clever ruse to outwit the maddened steer. The most disappointing part of it all was that my dear husband had not even seen my sorry plight, so did not offer me his sympathy.

My reason for telling this episode is to emphasize the fact that we ranch wives were liberated a long time before we had even heard of Women's Lib. Most of us enjoy working outside and would rather help out, if we can, than to put up with hired help. I know wives who are better ranchhands than most of the hired men you can get nowadays; but sadly, I don't qualify for that class. At best, I'm equal to some of the worst help you can hire, but then, I'm not an extra plate at the table either; and my one redeeming feature is that I can't quit when the going gets rough or the boss gets mad. I just sit down somewhere and cry a bit and then get up and go at it again. It works wonders, and things usually turn out fairly well after that.

Not that we haven't had hired men. We have! That's the reason I was out helping to catch that locoed steer. I had said I'd rather do the work myself than put up with any more hired men. Over the years we've had some dillies. It's always a good topic of conversation when neighbors get together and compare hired men.

When a rancher has to have extra help and picks up men in town, usually at a local bar, broke and hung-over, he never knows just what he and his family are getting into. Sometimes, too, these "floaters" will phone you for a job, usually late at night after you've gone to bed, and pour out their hard luck stories. All the while you can hear laughter, the tinkle of glasses, and music from a juke box in the background. They usually get a list of local ranchers and just go down the list phoning until someone hires them. Sometimes it doesn't work out very well for any of the partics involved.

Take the case of an old friend of mine who hired a man who studied all the sadistic crime magazines and boasted how he was smart enough to commit the perfect crime and get away with it. He tried to poison the boss, but my friend became suspicious when the food didn't taste right and he dumped it out. The hungry sheep dogs gulped it down and died agonizingly. There was no proof of the perpetrator at the time, but eventually the man was convicted after shooting and killing a man in the neighborhood and attempting to shoot another.

Another friend of ours had a pretty fair hired man who had worked there for years. He had been to our place several times and helped with branding and such and was always very clean and polite to be around. Then one day he shot another rancher's hired man in a silly squabble over a bottle of booze.

There was another fellow who had worked all over Blaine County and was considered to be very clean, quiet and conscientious. He did well when he worked for us, but the kids were deathly afraid of him because of his oddly white-ringed eyes. Then one night, he shot and killed a man who worked for one of my relatives. They had been drinking.

Of course, you cannot blame all this violence onto them by saying that they were barbarous and uncultured. Even the piano tuner we hired one summer didn't turn out to be any better. He seemed to be quite a nice person and spent one whole hot afternoon tuning our old family heirloom. He even offered to buy it at a very tempting price. His father before him had been a piano tuner and they had built up a very well-known business and reputation, with the son now restoring antiques on the side. He visited pleasantly with us while I gave him a lunch, little knowing that only three months later he would be locked in a psychopathic ward for shooting his young son while the lad lay sleeping.

John used to hate going to the bunkhouse to call one young man to breakfast. I never learned what the fellow feared, but he certainly was prepared for the worst. He kept a complete arsenal around his bed, all within easy reach. I was thankful when he left.

One dark spring night, I was alone at the place since John had gone somewhere and would not be back until late. The kids were all tucked into bed early, and I was nervous about the guy in the bunkhouse whom we had recently hired. He acted too familiar to suit me.

As so often is the case on a ranch, we didn't have any lock on the door of the house. I knew that sleep would be out of the question until John returned, although he had tried to persuade me that there was nothing to fear and that I should go to bed.

When still a young girl, I had learned that there is nothing so innocent looking and yet so effective as a hot iron to keep an amorous male at bay. So I resolved to stay up and iron until John came home. I always had plenty of ironing to do. I could have ironed all night if need be.

But first, I turned off the yardlight. Next, I turned off the porch light and arranged a tin pail full of empty pop bottles which we use to feed the bum lambs, setting it close to the inside of the porch door where it would be bumped and warn me if the door was opened. Then, with only one kitchen light on, I attacked the huge pile of ironing with a false vigor, all the while reassuring myself that it was so late and there was absolutely no reason for the hired man to come to the house at that hour.

My husband had not been gone over twenty minutes, and my nerves were just beginning to become unstrung a little when I heard the loud crash of the tin pail being roughly shoved aside and the lamb bottles hitting the floor. My heart nearly stopped on the spot, but I continued to force the iron over the fabric with nerveless fingers.

The kitchen door opened and the hired man came in. I ironed on without looking up so that he wouldn't see how afraid I was. He gave the pretense of wanting a drink of colder water, but I knew there was plenty of water at the bunkhouse and, in March, it was certainly cold. I don't recall if I said anything to him or not, but I do know that he hung around for what seemed an interminable length of time, making inane conversation with himself. Surely, he must have thought I was the crazy one to be ironing so zealously at that time of night.

At last, he drifted back to his lair and I scurried to replace the bottles in the pail by the door. But I was through ironing for the night. My shaky knees gave out and I simply sat down and listened closely for sounds in the night until, at long last, John came home.

Unfortunately, this character proved too costly for us, and we had to fire him in less than ten days. John had advanced him money when he came, and when he left he still had not earned enough to repay us. But in that short time he managed to drive through the side of a pole corral, and had backed into a brand new metal shed which ripped open as with a giant can opener. The final straw came when he tipped over a good four-wheel drive pickup, smashing in the top, in the only hole around within a quarter of a mile.

We did get one hired man we liked and tried to locate again at different times but without success. He had his own car, so he left every Saturday night and I was free of him until Monday morning. The winning point about him was not the fact that he did his own washing in the laundromat in town, or that he was extremely quiet around the house. No, it was the fact that he seemed to enjoy eating all the foods we didn't care for.

He ate quarts and quarts of pickles and jams that we were tired of. Also, any stale cake or pie that was left on the table disappeared the same way. Even after a hearty breakfast, he would quietly reach over to a covered cake container kept on the table and help himself to some old cookies or whatever I was glad to get rid of. He ate anything and everything.

But he did have one odd quirk. He apparently had a terrible temper if anything went wrong with the machinery. I'd often hear him a quarter of a mile away, swearing and screaming at the top of his lungs above the noise of the tractor. Since we were never able to locate him again, we hoped his temper hadn't gotten him into trouble.

One summer a neighboring rancher I knew hired a young man fresh out of college back east who was very enthusiastic about learning every facet of ranching. From dawn to dark he rocketed about without ever accomplishing much. They dubbed him "The Diarrhea Kid" for the way he rushed, but at least he was never violent.

We have had men who were subject to seizures, fits of shakes, and one man who grinned constantly. It was rather wearing on the nerves until we learned that he had some sort of a metal plate in his head and the smiling grimace was involuntary and pitiful. Another man came with only one pair of trousers and so, after wearing the knees out stacking hay bales, he simply turned them around and wore them backwards. Some came with nothing and left with everything. That is, everything loose they could get their hands on to carry off.

Since we ranched forty-eight miles from the nearest town, I was obliged to do the washing for just about every hired man we had and, oh, how I hated it! I tried to tell myself all the Christian axioms about loving your neighbor, doing unto others, finding Christ in everyone, etc. Then I would survey the heaps of rank underwear, smelly bedding and filthy work clothes and would forget them all. One man had the audacity to tell me how he wanted his shirts ironed! Naturally, all this laundry was gratis.

There was one thing that all these hired men had in common and that was appetite, spelled with a capital "A"! They all could eat, once they got their stomachs conditioned to seeing food again.

They came thin and hung-over. Sometimes, one would not show himself outside the bunkhouse for two or three days until I wondered if he was still alive. Then, when I was away from the house, food would start to disappear from the refrigerator or the pantry. I could tell then that he was getting healed up and would be in for a regular meal soon. The first few days at the table were only experimental, but within a few more days, they could always eat enough for two or three men. Some were experts at the art of shoveling the food in while carrying on a non-stop monologue at the same time. Others were fond of saying how really great the food was at the last place they worked.

I suppose, in all fairness, I should say something about some of the really good hired men we've known. There were those who clumsily started supper if we were late coming from town, or even shut the baby chickens in when it started to rain. Some were as gentle as a lady with the rancher's kids, and we enjoyed having them around. One such fellow cut all the children's hair for the family where he worked, and did a fine job of it too.

When I was very small, I remember the hired men as being very mannerly. They never swore around the house, always scraped and carried their plates out to the kitchen and thanked or praised the cook for the meal. Frequently, they would bring candy bars back from town to us children or give us extra money at fair time. Some were like part of the family; they went places with us and we enjoyed having them in the house on a winter evening to play cards or listen to the radio.

But, to me, the most memorable of all hired men were the Mexican laborers who were around when I was a youngster. They rolled up in their blankets individually to sleep, and sprinkled red hot peppers generously over all they ate. Potatoes and gravy seemed too mild a dish for them without the red peppers blanketing it. My mother used to shudder at the free hand they had with the white syrup during wartime sugar rationing. They laced their coffee or cold tea (we had no ice) with liberal amounts and then failed to stir it up, leaving large globs in the bottoms of cups and glasses.

I thought they were a wonderful, happy-go-lucky bunch that always smiled and rattled along in a lingo that only the Spanish speaking boss really understood. Many amusing incidents arose over this language barrier. One little Mexican was particularly likable, so we took him with us to the county fair. We youngsters took him on a very wild ride that made his black hair stand out and he prayed loudly the whole time, invoking all the saints to preserve him.

Best of all were the peaceful evenings when the work was done and they would sit in the doorways of the bunkhouses at dusk, singing their fascinating and haunting tunes in their foreign tongue. Sometimes a lanky neighbor boy with a shock of unruly blonde hair would accompany them on an old guitar. He didn't know the words, but he could pick out the melody as they sang. I thought these were the most beautiful sounds I had ever heard.

Now, most of the ranchers who have extra men try to get a year-round married man. These couples are furnished with decent living quarters, utilities, meat, a vehicle to use on the ranch, a very adequate wage and ample time off. Some of these men actually have a better life than the boss, who has all the responsibilities to bear while pinching pennies, losing sleep and fighting his ulcers over worry about how to make ends meet.

Luckily, since our children have gotten older, we have been able to dispense with the hired men, and I count that as one of life's great blessings.

3

Salute to A Bearskin Rug and Rural Schools

"Choose knowledge rather than gold. . ."
Proverbs 8:10

Slowly they came at first and then faster and faster until the huge flakes of snow buried everything in sight. All day long the snow had fallen steadily, and by afternoon the wind had risen and was whipping it into great piles and drifts about the schoolhouse. At times, the wind-driven snow completely blotted out the landscape, making it impossible to see even the fence around the school yard. We had the lights burning all day.

At three-thirty, the parents arrived promptly and whisked their offspring away before the blizzard grew worse. Mom looked hopefully out the window from time to time, but by four-thirty she was resigned to the fact that no one was coming after us that day.

Mom was teaching us at the time, in a one-room school, only a little over three miles from our place. There were only three other families besides us and only five pupils in all.

The storm grew worse as the day wore on. Since it had

been grey and dark all day, nightfall came even more rapidly than usual. The temperature plummeted downward with a steady determination.

"Find a good book and let's make the most of it," Mom advised me cheerfully. "We have lots of water and the coalbin is full, so we'll make out. I've stayed in worse places than this before. At least we're warm here."

So I settled down in a chair drawn up beside the huge potbellied old stove and attempted to engross myself with a much read and re-read book from the library shelf, but I remember how black and staring all those big high windows seemed and how the wind howled and rattled the panes.

The schoolhouse was large, old and drafty, but we were comfortable by the old round stove. Our real problem was one of food, for we had very little. We had not expected to be stranded there overnight and the school was not equipped with a teacherage or any facilities for a teacher to live there. Until my mother had begun to teach, the families nearby had always boarded the teachers with them. Our noon lunch was gone. Mom ate very little, but I always managed to clean up everything during two recesses and the noon hour.

Luckily, at the time, the three other mothers and mine had gotten together and decided to take turns sending a hot dish along each day during the winter months so that the school could gain more points for its accreditation. Since we had no indoor plumbing, sidewalks or other conveniences, they had to take advantage of everything they could to keep our school rated well.

On this particular day, one mother had sent over a kettle of corn soup to be warmed up on the hot plate and, in her haste to get home, she had neglected to retrieve her kettle. The youngster had also left in a rush, forgetting it. We were fortunate that they had done so.

We warmed up a little of the soup for supper and ate it with the few crackers remaining in the sack, all broken and crumbly. There was not much of the soup left, and I remember Mom cautioning me that we should eat only enough to satisfy our hunger pangs for we would be even hungrier in the morning.

There was plenty of water in the well just outside the door, and I ran out swiftly and brought in another pail before complete darkness settled in. The blizzard was still raging and the icy pellets stung my face, blurring my vision. A person could not have been out very long without freezing to death.

The evening dragged on until nine o'clock, and later I realized that Mom must have been craving the quantities of hot black coffee she always drank after school and during the evenings at home. Of course, there was none at the school.

Along about nine, she suggested we bed down for the night as we were both tired. At home, we always had to get up early to do chores, eat a big breakfast and get to school in time for Mom to build a good fire that would warm up the building before anyone else came.

Since we were in the midst of preparations for our annual Christmas program, we had a rather mangy old bear rug at the school for use in one of the plays. Mom insisted that I use the rug, so I spread it out on the floor alongside the red-hot stove, removed my sturdy boots and, covering my shoulders with my parka, I tried to sleep. Mom curled up on her coat on the other side of the stove, but I'm sure she slept very little. The floor was hard and drafty, and she had to get up many times during the long night to replenish the fire.

I lay awake for a long time watching the flicker of firelight through a long crack in the side of the stove, and listening to the endless moan of the wind straining against the walls of the old schoolhouse. Sometime during the night, I awoke with my feet itching like crazy. Mom really had a hot fire going and my feet in their heavy woolen stockings felt as though they were about to burn up. I slept little after that for one side of me was too hot, the other too cold, and the bearskin rug began to itch as much as my wool socks did.

Morning loomed grey and still, with big snowbanks up to some of the windows. The wind had stopped, but the mercury registered twenty below.

Mom warmed up the remaining dregs of soup, thinned down with water, and cheerfully informed me that, "It does a person good to get a little hungry once in awhile."

Only two children came to school that day, one with a team and sled; but the other one was the important one whose mother had brought the hot dish for the day. I still remember smelling it all morning as we did our lessons, and how good it tasted at lunch time.

That afternoon when school was out, we went to the home of the youngster on the sled behind the spirited team. It was still very cold and the roads were impassable in many places. Late that same night, after everyone had gone to bed, the dogs raised a ruckus and a knock at the kitchen door announced another storm-weary visitor. It was the rural mailman.

He had left town over twelve hours earlier and had gotten only a few miles past the schoolhouse. He had spent the entire day shoveling himself out of a succession of snowbanks in his attempts to turn around and follow his tracks back to town. After going into the ditch about a half mile from the school, he managed to walk, in the pitch darkness of that deadly cold night, for at least a mile to the ranch house where we were staying overnight. They made him welcome and helped him on his way back to town the next morning.

The following afternoon we were able to get back to our

own home, but for the last two days of school that week, my mother and I were obliged to take saddle horses to get there. There was a barn in the schoolyard, as some of the others rode to school all the time, but even with the shelter, the horses were raring to head for home and their own barn after school each day.

In those days, people really put an effort into getting their youngsters to school, even if it meant long trips with teams, or shoveling endless hours to get a pickup out of a snowdrift. None of the children missed unless they were sick in bed. We seemed to be a hardy bunch, so none of us missed very many days of school.

They always gave out perfect attendance certificates at the end of each school year, and a surprising number of the youngsters attending county rural schools received them. They should have given awards to the teachers too, for the heroic efforts they performed in keeping school open in those days.

When my mother first began her teaching career as a young girl, she rode horseback to and from the school, which was six miles away. She taught a large number of students in all eight grades, ranging in age from five years to almost her own age, so she encountered many problems. Also, this school had no barn so her horse had to stand tied to a post in all kinds of weather. Needless to say, the trip home at night was a speedy one. She owned several very spirited Morgan horses, and must have cut quite a dashing figure in her riding skirt as she raced to and from school on her fine horses.

During the warm days of fall and spring, we were admonished to watch closely for rattlesnakes. The schoolhouse sat close to Rattlesnake Butte which, at that time, had many snake dens in it. We killed numerous rattlers in the schoolyard, finding them in the weeds, under planks, and even under the schoolhouse steps. One time, a horse ridden to school by one of the girls was bitten on the nose while he grazed, and subsequently died from the bite.

We were always watchful since we had all been raised in snake country and had all had many close calls with rattlers. I believe we all carried jackknives at an early age, possibly with the excuse that it might be handy in case of snakebite.

The neighboring ranchers occasionally lost a cow or two from snakebite; and one day when my sister was riding, her horse was bitten just above the front hoof. We immediately went to town for the necessary antivenin and administered it as soon as we reached home, but the horse was sick and lame for a long time and was not ridden for several months after that.

One close call I had with a snake happened on a lovely spring day when Mom allowed a classmate and me to take a book outside to study. With the book between us, we sat down next to the building, rested our backs against the wall and proceeded to ask each other the prescribed questions. We each heard a slight hissing sound, but thought the other was making the noise until, a few moments later, we leaned forward and looked behind us.

Directly behind where we were sitting was a baby rattler, partly hidden by the green grass just starting along the warm foundation of the schoolhouse. Mom was frantically called. She dispatched the snake with great haste (and a big stick), telling us how fortunate we were not to have been bitten, as the snake was poisonous, even though it was too young to have fully developed rattles.

Of course, many days were too cold to play outdoors, so we amused ourselves inside by playing "Cattlemen versus Sheepmen" which was a slight variation from the "Cops and

Robbers" we played outdoors. Mom was very lenient about letting us children draw on the old painted grey floor with chalk to mark our fence lines and boundaries, as it was easily wiped up. But how she ever stood the running gun battles and "Bang. Bang. You're dead!" coming from behind the piano or under her desk is beyond me. We certainly didn't need any special classes in physical education such as our own children have today. I'm sure many of those fifteen minute recesses must have seemed an hour long to Mom.

At least once a year, usually at Christmas time, she brought all the fixings and made taffy on the hot plate for us. Each of us got our share on a saucer and were allowed to pull it ourselves. We always washed carefully first, but even so, the resultant blobs of grey usually contained everything from dog hair to crayon bits. Nevertheless, the flavor of that taffy is a memory to cherish.

Thus were my grade school years at Ada School. Like any normal youngster, I disliked studying, but with so few children in school, we were a close group and had fine times.

My husband, as a boy, attended Faber School which was a one-room log building about fifteen miles farther back in the hills than Ada School.

Faber School was named after John's grandfather, Nicholas Faber, who donated the acre of land for the schoolgrounds. He also helped in the cutting of logs and in the actual building of the school. Besides serving on the first school board, Nick planted many trees in the yard around the small, steep roofed log building.

John walked or rode to school, and his faithful dog, Penny, generally followed him to wait patiently all day and return with him at night. One spring, she had a huge litter of pups underneath the schoolhouse which greatly displeased the teacher.

While the youngsters were supposed to be hard at work on their lessons, the sounds of thumping, whining and puppy talk came up through the old floorboards, causing the children to snicker and look about, always eager for any interruption. The teacher cajoled and threatened John alternately, but there just wasn't any way to get the litter out easily without chopping a hole in the schoolhouse floor. So there they stayed, and the kids enjoyed it more every day as the puppies grew and became noisier.

At last, the hubbub became too much for the teacher and she issued an ultimatum which forced John to crawl through a small opening in the crumbling foundation, wriggle on his stomach through the dirt until he could reach the puppies, and then back out with one or two at a time. Several trips were made under the building before he secured them all and bundled them on home with him.

Now I watch our children waiting at our mailbox, a quarter of a mile away, for the school buses that will whisk them away to their respective schools. One goes to the high school in town where her days are filled with basketball, bowling, archery, cooking, sewing, speeches, art, singing and physical education, besides her regular studies. The lower grade children take the bus to a consolidated rural school, and even they are laden down with books and possibly a lengthy term paper on such a scholarly subject as "The Roman Empire." With all the restlessness of youth today in their search for whatever it is that is lacking in their lives, I can't help but question whether or not these young children of ours are really so much more privileged than we were.

The country dances in the various little schoolhouses used to be a big social event in the ranchers' and farmers' lives, and I was sorry to see the end of them. The number of rural schools has greatly diminished now, and many of these former schoolhouses have been sold and moved away. An important link with the past disappeared with the country school.

Before rural electrification ran out our way, we used two big gas lanterns hung from the ceiling by hooks to light the schoolhouse at night for whatever activities were going on, be it the Christmas program, election night, or a dance.

The dances were very exciting and well attended. Benches were arranged along the walls, and the huge teacher's desk, more like a table, was pushed into one corner. When piled high with all the coats, it made a most excellent bed for all the sleepy little tots. Naturally everyone brought all their children, who just fell asleep when they got tired and didn't bother anyone.

While the musicians took a break, it was great sport for the youngsters to slide on the floor which was made very slippery with cornmeal. At supper time, about midnight, there were large quantities of homemade doughnuts, sandwiches, pickles and cake, along with coffee, that all the women brought.

This was before Women's Lib, so only the man had to pay a small fee to get in; and he received a little ribbon to pin on his shirt front to show that he had paid. All ladies and children came free. Sometimes the lunch was free, as everyone donated it, unless they were raising money for some worthy cause. Then, a small charge was made per plate.

The dances were very orderly, perhaps because of all the small folks there to take everything in with big eyes and ears. The men were most courteous, removing hats and coats and politely asking the lady of their choice to dance, then returning her to her seat with a "thank you" afterwards. Occasionally, the musicians went outside with other men to "wet their whistles" and have a smoke, but there was no drinking in the hall, and anyone who imbibed too much was steered outside by a couple of conscientious local gentry.

Recently, my husband and I had occasion to attend a dance, and it made me sad to think that our children will never be able to enjoy good dances such as we used to have. At this dance nearly everyone was drunk and even the musicians were cordoned off by drink glasses, most of them emptied swiftly between dance tunes.

The young men nearly all wore their hats or, lacking a hat, a cap. Many wore heavy coats or insulated vests, even though the building was stuffy hot and rank with cigarette smoke. I noticed that the girls looked as if they had been cut from the same mold, having long stringy hair, wearing levis, and going about asking whomever they pleased to dance with them. Many were smoking and whenever they were done, they simply ground out the cigarette on the floor with the toe of their boot. No lunch was served, which might have helped to soak up some of the alcohol.

My freshman year in high school was also very memorable. Since I was only twelve when it came time for me to enroll in high school, Mom was most reluctant to board me in town. So she accepted a teaching position on an Indian reservation at the public grade school, and sent me to the nearby Mission School operated by the very good and capable Franciscan Sisters. There were only twenty-nine students in the entire high school, taught by two nuns and a priest, but the curriculum was full.

The school was very old and dignified, and had behind it a long and colorful history. The Sisters did a most magnificent job with the hundred and fifty students who comprised the grade and high schools. I was the only white student. I was a minority of one. However, it was a good year filled with many fine times. The Sisters kept up an interesting round of school activities which included debates, plays, carnivals, parents' nights, and contests of all sorts interspersed with the numerous church doings.

The events of that school year alone would fill a book; but here I will recount only one happening, but one that made a deep impression on my young mind.

Sometime during the winter when the weather was at its worst and the gravel road to the nearest town forty miles away was blocked, an important member of the Indian tribe passed away. The Sisters sat up all night at the Indian's home and prayed with the family. I don't believe the body was embalmed; but a casket was provided, from where I don't know.

Of course, the entire high school turned out to sing the Requiem High Mass, for if you were in high school, you were automatically in the choir. The coffin arrived at the little church loaded in the back of a pickup with flapping tire chains clanging a dirge of their own.

We sang the solemn service, and then the priest, the altar boys, the entire congregation and the school walked behind the same pickup to the nearby cemetery. As we stood there in the biting cold, shivering and watching the casket being lowered with lariat ropes into the grave, I remember noticing that all of the altar boys wore western boots without overshoes as they stood ankle deep in the snow around the grave.

Yes, I was a minority of one that school year, but we all got along very well. I was never made to feel like an outsider, which I was, and they accepted me most graciously, both at school and by inviting me into their homes. I cannot understand all of this racial and religious violence that abounds so freely in the world today.

I had a first hand experience of what it is like to be different from all the others, and yet I was treated fairly and as an equal. They could have made my days there a nightmare, but instead, the Indian students accepted me with Christian charity. I can truly look back with nostalgia on that freshman year at St. Paul's Mission in the Little Rocky Mountains.

4

Things I've Learned the Hard Way

"Plans fail when there is no counsel. . ."
Proverbs 15:22

I stood poised at the top of the hill with butterflies churning a drumbeat in my stomach. It was too late now to back out. I *had* to do it. My audience waited expectantly with worshipful looks on their shining young faces.

The fifty-five gallon metal oil barrel resting on its side at my feet was rust-flaked, dented and filled with cobwebs. It certainly didn't look like a reliable means of transportation to the bottom of the hill, but that was just what I intended it for.

"Hurry up! Come on!" the others jeered at my hesitation. "You said you'd do it!"

With a swaggering bravado I didn't feel, I crouched down and cautiously put my feet inside the filthy barrel, then drew the rest of myself inside. There was plenty of room, so I braced myself against the dirt-encrusted sides and ordered my cohorts to "let 'er rip!"

The barrel rolled slowly at first, with a scraping sound of gravel on the hilltop. Gradually it gained momentum until everything was a blinding whirl encompassed within the earsplitting sounds of rocks grinding underneath.

We hit an obstruction, and my swift moving barrel rose high into the air, leaped several feet, came down with a definite thud and continued on its erratic course downward at an even greater speed.

My whirling flight was punctuated by clamorous thumps and scrapings as we bumped downward at an alarming speed. The young spectators were following in my wake with gleeful shouts and praise, but I was oblivious to all except the seemingly endless whirling and noise.

Finally, when the barrel had rolled out onto the flat, lost its momentum and gradually rocked to a standstill, it was a very sick and shaky girl who sprawled half in and half out, with head ringing and images reeling.

The youngsters kept up their demands, "Do it again!"

But I turned a deaf ear on their lamentations and eased myself off toward the barn to recover my equilibrium. If there is a better way to come down a hill in a barrel, I never learned of it, nor did I ever try it again.

You might say that I graduated from the University of Adversity and, though it was rigorous, it was not without its lighter side.

For instance, there was the time that I was absolutely going to die if I didn't get to watch my three nephews wrestle in a state tournament. The situation was complicated by the fact that the tournament was being held in a city two hundred miles away and I had two very nice young bum lambs which needed feeding four times a day.

The problem was solved when the lambs went along to the tournament! They were warm in a roomy cardboard box on the floor of the back seat of the car. We took two large thermos jugs of hot water and some condensed milk with us to feed them.

Whenever feeding time approached, I simply dashed out to the car, poured milk about halfway up in the bottles and finished filling with the hot water. The lambs drank greedily and were satisfied when I again covered their box and rushed back to the tournament. Though they lived in that dark box in the car for twenty-four hours, they suffered no ill effects and never even bothered to bleat.

The lambs became quite the joke at the tournament, with many people stopping to ask me about them. Some asked me to bring them indoors, but I refused, not wanting trouble with the officials. We made the local news with "Loyal Lambs Go to Tourney" but it was well worth the effort and ribbing involved. The lambs grew into fine specimens which more than paid for the trip to the tournament.

At one time, I used to buy quite a few calves from a dairy thirty miles away. Whenever I'd get a call saying they had a calf for me, I'd take the back seat out of the car, throw in some plastic drop cloths, pack up whatever youngsters were underfoot at the time and dash off to get the calf.

Once I was unusually fortunate in securing a husky Holstein that weighed over a hundred pounds. The dairyman tied the calf's legs together with twine, but halfway home he kicked himself free and stood up. We happened to be driving through the town of Chinook just then, and we caused several near-accidents as I tried to drive along nonchalantly with the huge black and white head peering out of the back side window!

My son hung over the seat and chortled happily to the calf

during the ride, trying to feed it from his dripping baby bottle. I was doing just fine, I thought, until I rounded a sharp corner too fast and the rear door flew open. Out went the calf! I braked to an abrupt halt and backed up. The calf lay in a bewildered heap in the road and it took quite a bit of persuasion on my part to convince him to climb back into the car.

Our daughter, Jody, is very fond of bringing her pet rabbits into the house for her younger brothers, Elgin and Luke, to play with. I'll never forget the time she brought in two identical baby rabbits while I was making supper.

In the ensuing confusion, one rabbit got away and crawled into a very narrow crack between the wall and the breakfast bar. The bar is quite large, heavy and built into the floor, so there was no way of moving it. I was sure the tiny creature would never back out but would keep pushing forward. While the smaller kids wailed over their loss, I foresaw the slow death of the rabbit and the resultant odor.

At last, John came in and, like a truly resourceful man, he looked the situation over and acted without hesitation. He took a wire coat hanger and fashioned it into a long hook. This he slowly inserted into the narrow opening for two feet and moved it about cautiously until he was able to "hook" the bunny out.

Needless to say, the kids were most grateful and happy to have the pet back. They also were more careful after that when they brought them indoors.

Sometime back, when we had but two tiny baby girls, we gave a grand outdoor barbecue. It was a swell party on a warm summer evening in the beautiful Bear Paw Mountains. In fact, the party was such a huge success that fourteen people stayed overnight. Finally, my husband and I took the girls and adjourned to the bunkhouse, leaving the boisterous revelers to have the entire house to themselves.

But during the early course of the evening, someone spotted a beaver ambling along a stand of quaking aspen growing beside the small creek below our house.

With shouts, the whole crowd took off to chase the beaver. Not wanting to be left out of the fun, I grabbed up a youngster under each arm and sped after the fleeing mob. John and another young man were standing on the beaver's tail when I got within sight. It was hilarious to see two grown men trying to balance on a moving beaver's tail, for the poor frightened beaver was still making rapid tracks to leave the country, despite his passengers. It looked like a new kind of surfing or skate-boarding.

Of course, they didn't hurt the beaver, and they soon left him to go on about his business. Later, the group couldn't decide which was the funnier sight, the men on the beaver's tail, or me running downhill with a child under each arm, trying to catch up. That is the only party we ever gave that was crashed by a beaver.

I seem to have an affinity for doing the opposite of what others expect of me. I'm forever forgetting to wait for my change in stores until the clerk calls me back. I'm usually about two years behind on the date when I go to write a check. While I'm having difficulty figuring out the stamp machine, I notice very young children rush up to it, pause a moment and dash off with a fistful of stamps! Candy machines get balky as soon as I insert a coin, and parking meters get greedy when I turn the handle and nothing happens.

For years I've had appliances that gave me, but no one

else, terrific shocks. My washer used to give me 110 volts periodically, whenever it felt in the mood, until I took to wearing rubber gloves and overshoes whenever I approached it. Once it shocked me so bad that I was numbed from my fingertips to my shoulder for a time and, at that same instant, I developed an intense headache. Then my electric mixer picked up the same little trick. I approached it with great caution, but my young daughters could use it without any problem whatsoever.

The final straw came when my new electric stove began shocking me whenever I lifted a pot lid. It got so I was afraid to even lift the coffee pot without first acknowledging my unworthiness to my Creator. I expected to meet Him almost any day! No one else was bothered by the stove.

Maybe you've come to the conclusion that I have no kinship with mechanical devices. If so, you're absolutely right. I'm the type who has had three flat tires within half an hour. I've wrecked more gas tanks, and have been seen speeding along, leaving a wet trail while trying to reach some place, any place, before all the gas ran out. I'm the type who loses a muffler on a rickety bridge and hangs up until someone's hired man happens along to unhook me.

When I have a flat tire, you can automatically assume one of two things. One, the spare tire will be flat; or two, the jack will break. Cars simply *do not* like me. The starter will stick for me and no one else. I'm the only one in the family who can park along a very low curb and still break the valve stem off and lose all the air in my tire.

My trouble with automobiles really began seventeen years ago. One bright, green-gold spring morning I went out to get some papers from the back seat of our Mercury which was parked on a steep incline by our house. I got the necessary material and was walking away, leaving the car door open for another trip, when the car suddenly began to roll backward down the hill. It struck me. The open car door hit me, pinning me against the side of a parked jeep. I believe the only thing that saved me was the fact that I was crushed against the spare tire bolted to the side of the jeep.

But what really saved me was that my mother happened along with her rural school children on a field trip. She was horror-stricken and the children stood solemnly about as she eased the front door open and slid into the driver's seat. The weight of the Mercury pinning me against the jeep on the hillside was excruciating, but I still remember that extra torturing pressure when Mom got into the car and drove it ahead to release me.

Certainly, I would have died if I'd had to undergo the pain and pressure all day long until my husband returned late at night. The doctor could find no injuries, but my body took on the coloring of army camouflage. Since that day, I've never trusted any vehicle parked on a slope, even though it is in "park" or left in gear.

I also learned at a young age that I would never make a roper. I used to practice with my sister by the hour and, though she reached a fair degree of success, I was a failure. The one time I did catch a critter was nearly the end of me.

My sister, Joan, and I had gone out to check some registered cattle for pinkeye. Since we had halter-broken all the calves at weaning time, we went with the pickup, planning to catch anything on foot that needed doctoring. We did find a yearling heifer that needed some medicine put on her eye, so we stopped the pickup and I got out with a lariat and lots of optimism. Unfortunately, I snared her the first try, but she spooked and took off in a high lope.

Somehow, my foot became entangled in the rope and I

was jerked off my feet and dragged along on my back after her for some distance. I only hit the high spots, but it did seem they were the ones covered with sharp rocks and cactus. Later on, it was a funny experience; but at the time, I came to the conclusion that perhaps my talents lay in fields other than roping!

Recently, I had a check to cash and, as I happened to be in town early one Saturday morning, I walked into a local bank. The place was deserted except for two workmen in an ell off the vestibule. I stood on first one foot and then the other waiting for the bank personnel to come on the scene. I realized I was early, and perhaps they were still putting away coats, plugging in the percolator or whatever they did first thing in the morning since this was a small town bank.

I began to notice that the workmen were peering at me around the corner every few minutes. I was flattered. I straightened up a bit, sucked in my stomach, fluffed out my hair and then I got a glimpse of myself in the mirror on the opposite wall. No, I decided, they definitely were not ogling me! It had been some time since I could honestly say I'd been ogled at. Deflated, I sauntered over to watch what they were doing. They appeared to be knocking a large hole in the beautiful yellow wall. I looked on and they kept working, glancing up suspiciously at me from time to time.

After a bit, I began to feel conspicuous, so I thought it would be fine to strike up a conversation.

"Say," I began with a nervous titter, "Aren't you working on the wrong side? I thought people were supposed to break *in*, not *out*! Ha–ha."

They glanced at each other again with inscrutable looks. Then one rose and towered over me in his white coveralls.

"Can I help you, Ma'am?" he asked with a frown.

"No thanks," I answered him pleasantly, "I'm only waiting for the bank help to show up and cash a check."

"Bank's never open on Saturdays," he declared doubtfully with stony eyes fixed on me. "We're just repairing here."

I mumbled something and beat a hasty retreat in embarrassment, leaving two puzzled workmen looking after me.

One night I was awakened by the dog barking outside. After a time, I got up to investigate without disturbing John, who is able to sleep through almost any commotion. I didn't turn on any lights, but peered out of the window into the inky black countryside in the direction where the dog was barking his head off.

I could see something tall and white out there! It looked like a person walking up our muddy road. I assumed that someone had had car trouble and was walking in for help when stopped by our dog. So, I opened the door and called out.

"Who's there?"

Silence greeted me. Even the dog stopped barking, but the figure in light colored clothing was still standing there. I waited a bit and then repeated my question. Still silence. I was fast becoming irritated. Why didn't he answer me? Surely he could hear me!

Then the figure began moving slowly toward me again. I could hear the sloshing and slipping about in the water-filled ruts.

By now I was very mad, so I bellowed, "I can hear you and I can see you out there! What do you want?"

Immediately, the figure stopped again and stood stock-still for several long minutes while I lingered, shivering in my night clothes. Again no answer, and then I heard the sloshing of footsteps again.

Thoroughly aroused now, I shouted, "All right, let's take a look at you if you won't answer!"

I reached over and flipped on the yardlight.

There, standing in the muddy road within the circle of light, stood our tall old Holstein milk cow. What I'd been hollering at was the long white patch of hair that ran from her hip bone all the way down her leg to her hoof. In the dark, it did look very much like a person in light colored clothes. The rest of her, being black, didn't show up at all.

I switched off the yardlight and slunk sheepishly back to bed, grateful for the fact that John could sleep through Gabriel blowing his horn. I didn't want him to know I'd been interrogating the milk cow at two in the morning.

As a young girl, along about the time I began to notice boys in earnest, I became unusually absentminded. My mother could probably fill a book with tales of my forgetfulness and carelessness, but I'll only tell a little here.

One fine day, I was saddling up my horse to go for a ride. Naturally, my mind was on the upcoming dance on Saturday night. In those days, there were no such things as days of the week. The calendar read like this instead: *Saturday night,* blank, *Saturday night,* blank, *Saturday night,* blank, etc.

Anyway, I tossed my saddle on the horse's back. I caught the swinging cinch and pulled it up tight. Picking up the bridle reins, I turned around and headed for the barn door, fully expecting my faithful horse to be at my heels. I came to the end of the reins with a halt. My horse stood in the exact same position with his head turned and stretched out toward me.

I gave him a slight, impatient jerk and called to him. He didn't move, so I went back into the shadowy stall to investigate. It took me only a second to see what was wrong.

My cinch had gone over the divider in the stall and I had cinched my horse tightly to a pole! Fortunately, he was a patient beast and waited for me to unhook him instead of tearing down the barn.

Another time, I was raking hay with an Allis-Chalmers tractor and a side delivery rake. It was a beautifully clear, cool, summer day without wind. The past Saturday night dance had been more than I'd hoped for and I had great expectations for the next one. Thus, I went driving along blithely, singing at the top of my lungs and watching the hawks wheel overhead, searching for the mice I was uncovering in the windrows of hay.

I must have gone three hundred feet before I noticed something was wrong. I missed the accompanying scrape and grind of the rake. I glanced back and spotted my rake back down the hay field. The hitch had come loose and I had merrily gone on without even missing it. I stopped, backed up quickly, and was able to get hooked up again before anyone noticed my trouble and could ask where my mind was.

A good way to assemble a crowd fast, we learned, is to burn something down. We used to have a ramshackle old chicken house and several smaller dilapidated old buildings which we wished to dispose of. They were definite eyesores. So we waited for the right time.

John decided that when all the neighbors would be at the county fair would be an excellent time. So we piled all the old boards, tar paper and junk together and he lit a match to it. The flames licked greedily at the rotten wood and began eating away at the mess. The kids and I were out all afternoon, helping to drag up more junk. John became so pleased with his success at cleaning up that he had gotten his tractor to pull up more bigger and bigger objects to further feed the blaze.

We became so engrossed in our own personal holocaust that we didn't notice the approaching dusk. By then, the flames were leaping thirty feet into the air and visible for a great distance.

I was the first one to see the long string of car lights coming from up and down the valley at great speed, all headed to our place. John was too busy chewing tobacco, spitting, and happily piling more junk onto his roaring inferno to notice. He didn't hear the sounds of the car motors over the roar of the fire until I hollered at him. He turned around, shocked to see that most of our neighbors for several miles around had all turned out to fight fire!

Like good country people, they all took it good-naturedly and went home chuckling. However, we did stop feeding the blaze then, and waited anxiously through the long hours for our junk heap inferno to die down while we watched the road nervously. Indoors the girls were busy answering the phone, saying, "No, everything is all right. We don't have a fire."

You get out of life just what you put into it. I've heard it said that nothing is sure except death and taxes, but I'm sure of one other thing. As long as you are able to laugh with others at yourself, everything will turn out fairly well for you. You'll even be surprised at all the enjoyment you'll have too.

5

All God's Little Creatures

"And God made the beasts of the earth according to their kind. . ."
Genesis 1:25

"Caw! Caw! Caw!" came the raucous laughter of the big ebony bird preening himself atop his favorite perch on the coal house roof.

"That bird has got to go," muttered my mother as she stood in the kitchen door. "This is the last straw."

Mom was referring to the clothesline where she had only just completed hanging out a large washing of white dish towels, tablecloths and underwear. The snowy white wash, gleaming in the soft noonday sunshine, was now streaked with black muddy claw prints along the top where it was pinned to the line.

Oscar, as the family pet crow was named, had been a nuisance from the very beginning, but the kids loved him. He followed everywhere and his beady eyes missed nothing. Occasionally, he found a hen's nest and helped himself to the eggs until he developed such a liking for them that he went on frequent forages looking for eggs.

He was a villainous black thief with a greedy little heart beating within his shiny breast. He loved shiny things and would often sneak into the house in search of treasure whenever the door opened. He coveted any bright object and secreted many away, frequently leaving a bottle cap or something else in the place of a spoon that he had stolen.

He also had a fascinating side to his personality. He loved to make mud pies with the kids and go for long walks with them. He flew along, never getting too far ahead or behind, and kept up a running conversation. In short, Oscar loved company, but despite his adorable ways at times, he was nevertheless a blackguard.

A country child has many opportunities to own pets and to learn first hand the exciting and fascinating ways of old Mother Nature. I can pity the city-bred child who is so pinned to the television set or to a stack of comic books that he is oblivious to the real drama going on about him. A recent report I read showed that many city children could not identify even the common robin. How much they have missed in their concrete jungles!

Many have been the times I've had to run outside during the night to chase the deer out of the yard before they did damage to my shrubs and baby evergreens. Even with my careful vigil, they manage to come in and prune up all my young fruit trees every winter, and they come within ten feet of the door to check out the bird feeders.

As a youngster, I used to awaken to the flapping of the turkeys at daybreak as they left their perches high in the box elder trees where they were safe from marauding coyotes during the night. By the time the pink-grey dawn had changed into bright golden light, the turkey herd was far out ranging over the hills in search of grasshoppers and other insects. No one went about spraying indiscriminately in those days; there was no need to.

Many ranch kids have had pet skunks at one time or another. We only had them for one summer, and that happened quite by accident.

We had been losing chickens to skunks, so a careful watch was set up and two grown skunks were shot at the chicken house in a couple of nights. We thought the problem had been solved until we discovered, to our dismay, that the skunks had lived under the chicken house all the time and had raised four babies there.

There always were lots of cats around the hen house to clean up the mice that came to the grain, so the hens were not afraid of the cats, especially since some of them lived in the insulated hen house during part of the cold winters. We kept a cat dish there and every morning some of us took left-over hot cakes and milk to the cats after breakfast.

The first we knew of the baby skunks was when we saw them drinking milk from the cat dish. We had disposed of their mother, and hunger had driven the little ones out to search for food. They found it within four feet of the small hole that burrowed back under the building.

The irony of the situation was that, in ridding ourselves of two skunks, we gained four more. What could be done about the hungry little babies with their pointed faces and bright eyes? We did the natural thing. We fed them. We fed them every morning, and daily they grew tamer and tamer until we could pet them and scratch them on the stomachs which made them lie down. But we did treat them with healthy respect.

Since the chicken house was at some distance from our

house and the grass was tall, it was very disconcerting, to say the least, to have several small skunks pop out on the path ahead of you if you were a bit late in serving up breakfast in the mornings. Then they'd patter on ahead with tails held high to wait at the dish for the customary milk, hot cakes, and an occasional cold fried egg.

As the summer wore on, we wondered what to do with them. It is true that they answered to "kitty, kitty, kitty" and wandered peacefully about among the scratching hens. They even shared the same dish many times; but we knew the time would come when they realized just what sort of kitty they really were. You just can't have four skunks living with the chickens.

It was suggested that we sell them in Great Falls where they would be de-scented and sold as pets, but the idea didn't appeal to us. We could not feature these carefree little creatures locked in cages or mauled by children, even if it did sound like a lucrative business.

They added a bright spot of interest to that summer and repaid us by never once molesting a chicken, and never once did they smell up the place. The problem solved itself when they grew older and simply ran away to live like wild skunks.

Once we came upon one of them, or thought we did, in a hayfield and, although he was quite tame, he had learned a new wariness.

Today, with rabies so prevalent that skunk extermination programs have been implemented, I would not undertake to become friendly with one again. One of our children's classmates was bitten by a rabid skunk; and even though the boy fully recovered, I understand the treatment he underwent was far from pleasant.

Some friends of ours raised a baby raccoon they had found after its mother had been killed. It made the most adorable, fascinating pet I can think of, but it was also a mischievous little troublemaker.

Once, while we were visiting their home, Oscar, as the raccoon was named, decided he wanted John's soft fuzzy Scotch cap and he tried every way he could to get it away from John. Finally, John hung the cap on a hat tree, but no sooner had he sat down again than Oscar was up the hat tree like a streak after the cap. He did mind well though, for he came right back down when scolded by his mistress.

These same friends kept a dog in the house too, and the way that dog and raccoon would roll on the floor and wrestle was something to see. The coon was also very fond of making a big mess. Usually, he spent the daytime hours sleeping in an upstairs opened dresser drawer where it was quiet; then came out at night about the time his owners wanted to go to bed and get some rest. At that time of night, he was ready to have some fun, so he would scamper noisily over the entire house, inspecting everything and looking for something to get into.

If they were away during the day, he seemed to know it was safe to make a frightful disorder of things. Oscar played in the garbage can every chance he could, and if he was lucky enough to get hold of a facial tissue or paper, he would shred it up into tiny pieces which he scattered everywhere. He also loved to get into the ash trays and, after tearing open the cigarette butts, he would fling the tobacco bits about and grind the particles into the shaggy living room rug. He loved to smear up windows and pull on the curtains as well as any little tot I have known.

In fact, their house looked exactly as if they did have a tiny toddler about, for most of the kitchen cabinets were tied shut. With his great sense of smell, Oscar could ferret out cookies, bread, or whatever else tickled his fancy, and he could use his little paws, so much like tiny hands, to open almost any cupboard latch.

We watched him that day as he ate a snack. One of his favorite foods was fruit flavored dry cereal puffs, which were served to him in one half of a divided dish, with the other half containing a little water. It was a very merry sight to watch him using his paws to drop the round bits of cereal into the water, then fish them out with his paws to eat them. Of course, he did everything with enthusiasm, and it wasn't long before the kitchen floor was spotted with water drops, cereal crumbs and little wet raccoon tracks.

A goat is another good pet for a country kid. Robin Hood came into our lives when I was about nine years old. He was one of triplets, so our neighbor gladly gave him to me. I named him Robin Hood, who was my hero at the moment; but later the name changed to Robbie. He lived for many years and, throughout his entire life, remained the same intelligent, vain, attention-loving pet. He quickly learned to raise his foreleg and shake hands when asked to do so. He would also bow down for a lump of sugar. He was taught to jump on the backs of the 4-H calves and stand there like some regal monarch. He loved it, and the calves didn't mind either.

One day a 4-H tour went by our place, and although the leaders and county agent did their best to examine the calves and point out instructive features to the young club members, they wasted their breath in the empty air. The goat stole the whole show that day.

Contrary to popular opinion, goats do not eat anything and everything. They are very finicky and will taste only the best. From the tracks, we could ascertain that Robbie took an early morning tour every day through the garden, tasting a bit here and nibbling a bite or two there of the most luscious vegetables, before he would neatly scale the fence and follow the sheep out to graze.

Mom was very patient with all the creatures we children used to bring home. She put up with baby mice which we had found in a shed and kept in a coffee jar, feeding them with an old eye dropper. She put up with baby cottontails and a Hungarian pheasant that was crippled, which we cared for until it was able to fare for itself again.

Many were the long foolish hours I spent in trying to catch a live gopher for the ideal pet I envisioned it to be. At last, I came into possession of a hamster which was enough like a gopher to satisfy that longing. And it did not take long to satisfy that desire either, for that was the meanest-tempered, nastiest little thing I have ever seen. It quite literally bit the hand that fed it. Unless disturbed, it spent all of its time in a messy little nest.

We had pet chickens of all kinds. One was called Orphan Annie and was raised behind the kitchen stove in a box to keep it warm. It would snuggle up the sleeve of an old shirt and chirp quietly until it fell asleep. Soon it was big enough to go outside with the other chickens, and Mom was glad to see it go as we youngsters were fond of letting it roam around the house with us.

Old Lonesome was a huge white turkey gobbler that was neither very friendly nor very hostile. Usually, he was quite reserved, but sometimes he would follow us to the house and come right in the front door if invited to do so. There he would strut around the front room displaying his gorgeous white plumage. Before long, Mom would start to get nervous and make him go back outside before he decided to leave his calling card.

All in all, Mom was a very good sport and, remembering this, I try to have patience when my own son comes running in excitedly to tell me he's caught and penned up three

gophers. Usually, he turns them loose within half a day because, as he explains, "They didn't like it in there." And I try to remain calm when my daughter says, "I didn't think you'd mind, Mom, but I put the buck rabbit in with the does *yesterday*!"

Besides horses, most ranch kids have a steer or a milk cow calf that they can saddle up and ride. We used to think it fine sport to "buck" out the milk cows, but that was usually frowned upon by the adults who were concerned about the detrimental effect this would have on the vital cream check, so it had to be performed in secret, usually after the evening milking was over. Big buck sheep and pigs are all very difficult to ride; yet, country kids all over still keep on trying to do it.

To ranch folks, horses belong in a category by themselves. They not only perform a necessary service and provide pleasure, but become a real companion. Every child falls in love with his first old nag, commonly a retired cow horse, and vows that it is the best horse in the world. These retired cow horses sometimes render a good service in training the young riders how to work around stock.

From years of experience, the old horses know how to head off a cow, and how to watch so the calves don't turn back. They are sensible, keen, and usually are a big help in moving cattle, regardless of what the young cowboy astride is doing or looking at. In time, the child learns more and moves on up to a more spirited horse that can cover more ground and accomplish more. Any child with a gentle horse, regardless of its beauty or worth, is a fortunate child indeed.

I remember the time an eighth grade boy led his horse up the wooden steps and through the door into the small entry of our rural schoolhouse. The young schoolteacher became quite upset as the floor seemed weak; the horse was most reluctant to turn around, and absolutely refused to back out and down the steps. Finally, after the rest of us school children cleared out, making more room, he was able to turn his animal around and lead it out.

Naturally, dogs and cats flourish in the country with no leash laws or city pounds. The cats multiply around the barns and out-buildings, raising a couple of litters a year, but they also keep the mouse and gopher population down. Over the years, we have had many worthwhile house cats too; but now I am told that, due to rabies and another disease with a hideous name, it is too risky to keep cats as house pets. I'm glad we didn't know this years ago.

Dogs are perennial favorites and truly man's best friend as the multitude of dog books in any library will prove, so I will not dwell for any length here, except to say that some of my favorites have been sheep dogs. I have seen these highly intelligent dogs perform many wondrous feats. Once well-trained and devoted to their master, there is hardly any limit to what they can do.

I knew of one that would catch and hold a ewe on command, and again jump in to kill either a rattlesnake or skunk that he felt might be a threat to his master. Another big old brown and battle-scarred dog would get up and growl, ready to do battle, whenever you said, "Coyotes! Pete!" He was ready to defend the band at a mere word, and that took real courage for I know of instances when the coyotes have lead dogs off by trickery and killed them.

There is a world of difference between the lonely sentinel on the hilltop with his master, watching over a band of sheep, and the spoiled little poodle that gets his regular clipping and perfuming. Yet, they each fill a need. Whenever the circumstances allow, I think every child should have a dog. A youngster who learns early in life to be kind to animals will grow up to be kind to his fellowman. Much can be added to a child's education by the responsibility of caring for a pet, even if it be only a goldfish.

I believe that children should be taught early to understand and enjoy the birds around us, if only the common sparrows, starlings or pigeons. Bird watching can open up a fascinating new world for young and old alike.

Here on the ranch, we have encouraged the birds for many years, for we appreciate the valuable assistance they lend in keeping the insect population down, besides the pleasure they give us. In winter, we shudder at the seemingly tons of sunflower seeds we have to buy, but we feel the cost is worth the benefits. On cold winter days, we keep up to twelve bird feeders well-stocked with suet, sunflower seeds, homemade doughnuts on a string, and a log drilled with holes which are filled with a combination mixture of peanut butter, cooked rice, ground grain and melted fat.

A favorite food relished by most birds is bird cake. Bird cake is made by mixing up two cups of flour, a spoonful of baking powder, a dash of sugar or honey, whatever melted fat is handy, and enough water to make a thick dough. This I spread into a greased cake pan and bake at 375° until done and crumbly. It is a most excellent feed, especially if prepared with whole wheat flour.

We try to keep something out for all types of birds, and we're rewarded in winter by a constant stream of birds to our yard all day long. Their gay chatter makes one think that winter cannot be so long and cold after all, for they are here every day, regardless of the weather. It is important to keep the feeders filled for, after a bitter cold night, they will need to find food at the first crack of day as their rapid metabolism makes it imperative for a bird to eat very often.

Don't fear that you'll be raising a bunch of free-loaders. Even while they await their turn at the feeders, they are busy searching the tree trunks, shrubbery, and along the eaves of the house for any beetle or insect egg. In the summer, few come for a handout unless it is a weary female having a hard time finding enough food fast enough to fill up her hungry brood. During the summer, these friendly, tame birds are busy ranging over the fields and over our huge garden, taking care of the pest problems for us.

We shall never forget one little chickadee. We named him Dumb-Dumb because of his slowness to learn. It was summertime and rarely do the chickadees come into the yard then, for they are off rearing their young in tall trees in solitary places. During the colder months, we can whistle them in, but during the summertime we could whistle our heads off and they couldn't care less. They're too busy eating the plentiful food that nature supplies them.

One certain day, we all heard the cry of an anguished bird through the opened windows. As the noise continued, we looked out and saw a full-sized young chickadee sitting on a branch a few feet from the window feeder where a thin and molting little female was searching for the seeds that had been kept there during the winter. Quickly, I took out a handful of sunflower seeds and we watched that patient little mother crack seed after seed and put the kernel in the fledgling's open mouth.

We had a ringside seat for nearly five days as every day the harried little mother brought the big fat youngster to the feeder, trying to fill him up and still his cries. Sometimes the male joined her in cracking seeds and feeding the baby.

The only time Dumb-Dumb would shut his bill and stop his demanding racket was when he swallowed a sunflower seed kernel. This kept up every day until we had almost given up on the bird brat ever learning to feed himself. Finally, the day arrived when the poor parents could not bring the food fast enough to suit him, so he hopped over and took a seed for himself and proceeded to crack it.

I can imagine that the tired little mother must have been very relieved when he did so. I think the parent birds must have been hard put to keep their baby's insatiable hunger stilled, or they would never have ventured into the summer-time bedlam of our yard when none of the other chickadees were about.

We don't know whatever became of Dumb-Dumb after he learned to feed himself, but we suppose he is one of the flock that comes every day to eat during the cold months when the wind howls, the snow blows, the mercury drops, and the chill factor gets to sixty degrees below zero. On a day such as this, their song is worth the cost of the feed and the labor involved.

It is very soul-lifting on a dull winter morning to see and hear a whole flock of waxwings in the nearby treetops, or to see a platoon of red cross-bills occupied with cutting up sunflower seeds only a few feet from the window. Bird watching is also a good pastime for the children when sickness confines them to the house, for they will sit for hours in a comfortable spot near a window and watch the endless antics of the birds. Even the most restrained person who claims no interest in birds will eventually get that amused look on his face during a meal here at the ranch. You can feel his attention straying and, finally, out comes the inevitable, "What kind of a bird is *that* out the window there?"

Usually, a pair or two of wild Canadian geese nest in a sheep pasture not far from the house and, in spite of the large number of foxes and coyotes, they sometimes manage to raise a few young ones. We know spring is finally here when we hear the first of the wild geese going over and hear their calling. I always think they're arguing about directions, but perhaps they only like to make conversation as they fly along and look down upon the rest of us.

The woodpeckers and chickadees are the easiest to tame. However, they are also very selective and very demanding. They'll let you know loudly when the feeders need filling or when a cat is up a tree.

We have a bevy of cats here, but thus far things have gone along fairly well. The large number of cats sitting about on our doorstep does not seem to diminish the number of birds coming to our feeders. One time, John did have to nail a strip of tin around the bottom of a tree where a robin had nested because every few hours the poor robins would raise a clamor until one of us went out with a broom to chase away a cat that was trying to climb up the tree to the nest. After the tin was in place, the robins went ahead and raised four fine youngsters.

Starlings are not much of a bother since there is plenty of grain spilled around the granaries and in the livestock feed troughs for them to eat. Also, the wild pheasants come to the feed ground and pick up grain and seeds from among the cattle. They soon learn if John is feeding oat hay, and become daily visitors then.

Neither do sparrows make a nuisance of themselves. They usually eat with our tame pheasants and so leave the bird feeders for the other birds to use. We raise the beautiful, exotic, red and multi-colored Golden Heritage pheasants as a hobby. Under state law, we are licensed and obliged to keep the pheasants confined in wire pens. However, the wire pens pose no difficulty to the sparrows and they go right through to help themselves to the cracked corn put out for the pheasants.

Suddenly, on some bright, clear morning, I smell spring in the air. The clear call of "ok-a-lee" announces the arrival of the first blackbirds. Under the dark earth, I can sense the faint stirrings of life as the cycle renews itself. The very air feels fresh and clean and I feel like shouting to the whole world the word from Ecclesiasticus, "Look upon the rainbow, and bless Him that made it!"

6

"Mom's Over in the Sheepshed"

"Love not sleep, lest poverty oppress thee. . ."
Proverbs 20:13

The organist was just starting the opening bars of a lovely inspirational hymn as I slipped unobtrusively into a pew as near the back of the church as I could get. The congregation stood, bedecked in their Sunday splendor, with voices and hearts uplifted as the music swelled and then faded away.

We sat. As the pastor's voice droned sonorously on, I caught myself nodding and my eyes closing. The church was too hot and too crowded. I'd had only four hours of sleep the night before and that had been broken up by my nightly sojourn to the lambing shed.

I know I was dozing when, suddenly, a small crawling sensation on the back of my neck electrified me. I jerked erect and thrust up an inquiring hand. My searching fingers produced only an offending bit of fur from the collar of my coat. My pulse settled back to normal, but I remained awake during the rest of the service. The thought of a sheep tick crawling on my neck was enough to fully arouse me from my lassitude.

During lambing time, I spent days and nights in the lambing shed helping with the sorting of sheep, feeding of hay and grain, hauling water to the penned up animals and assisting with the difficult deliveries. Any orphaned lambs, or any twin or triplet lamb that a ewe couldn't raise, I raised by feeding them milk from pop bottles five times during every twenty-four hour period. These were called the "bum" lambs.

I also painted big black corresponding numbers on all the ewes and lambs to avoid any mix-up when they were turned out together in large bunches. This involved a lot of work, crawling over fences with messy paint buckets and metal numerals which I used to dip in the paint and put the numbers on the sheep. Even with gloves, I always managed to get the sheep paint in my hair and firmly embedded in my hands during the month we were lambing.

But on Sunday mornings, it never seemed to fail. I always got up extra early to have plenty of time to get the shed work out of the way before preparing for church. Then, as I took a last walk through the "drop band" (ewes that hadn't dropped a lamb yet), I'd spot at least one ewe, wild as the wind, and with the lamb coming in a breech position.

This always entailed a wild run until I could catch the ewe and pull the lamb. By the time I had breathed life into the wet and listless lamb and had them safely confined in a lambing "jug", I would invariably have only five or ten minutes at the most to get dressed for church. I always managed a hasty shower, even if I didn't have time to do more than brush the alfalfa leaves out of my hair.

So I always lived in fear on Sunday mornings that somewhere I had missed a sheep tick! These ticks are really harmless, but have a repugnant appearance due to their large size, grey color, numerous legs and their ability to bite hard and leave large red welts. I knew that few of the city people in our church would recognize a nice fat, healthy sheep tick if they saw one, and would be horrified if they saw one on me. Sunday morning services were never relaxing.

On this particular morning, more asleep than awake, I had neglected even taking a hymn book. The beautifully groomed woman next to me sidled over and extended her book for me to share. She gave me a lovely smile and my heart warmed toward her as I put out my hand to take one side of the book.

Then I stopped and stared. Her long tapering crimson-painted nails complemented her lovely soft white hands adorned with glittering rings. My own hand, halted in mid-air, was red, rough and chapped, with torn fingernails, a long angry red welt where I had been caught on some barbed wire, and stained with the vestiges of black sheep paint that I had been unable to scrub off. I withdrew my hand miserably, leaving her to hold the book for the both of us.

I knew this woman slightly and, although she was a very nice person, she would not have understood what it was like to work night and day in a lambing shed. I consoled myself with the thought that Jesus had been born in a stable and His first visitors had been shepherds who came in haste; so perhaps they had not had time to dress nicely. Just *possibly* one of them *might* have had a sheep tick on his person too! That thought cheered me and I was able to smile wearily when one of the Biblical passages for the day turned out to be, "I am the Good Shepherd. I know mine and mine know Me."

I thought of that passage later as I walked to the shed after church, once more in my working clothes, to feed my herd of forty-eight bum lambs. They certainly did know me too! They heard me coming with bottles clanging from a hundred feet away, and set up a clamor inside their metal shed that threatened to deafen me. I smiled to myself, thinking that I now knew how movie stars and other celebrities felt when beseiged by a loving but howling mob, for the lambs could only be described as a loving, howling mob.

I always kept the bum lambs separated in pens holding no more than seven lambs each. Every pen had its own heat lamp and pan of grain and pellets. In theory they were confined; but, in their excitement over the prospect of warm milk, there were always some that could either jump over or "leak" through the fences.

To feed them I use two pails, one containing pop bottles already filled with milk, and the other filled to the brim with milk for refilling the pop bottles as they're emptied. I use a wooden rack that hangs over the fence, in which seven bottles will lay at the proper angle for the lambs to suck without being able to pull off the rubber nipples. This rack is a vast improvement over the way I used to feed lambs, holding the bottles by hand. In that way, I could feed only two or possibly three lambs at a time. It also avoids the back strain caused from bending over. Now I can stand up and watch them drink.

Some of the more up-to-date sheepmen are using self-feeders to rear their extra lambs. These self-feeders are filled once every day with cold milk. The idea being that lambs will help themselves whenever they wish to, and the coldness of the milk will prevent them from drinking too much at one time.

I'm too old fashioned. I like to see how much each lamb takes at a feeding. Feeding time also gives me a good

opportunity to check each lamb over and appraise his condition, health-wise. This is the ticklish part of raising bum lambs, for I believe they must be treated much like human babies in order for them to grow up and return their owner a profit.

Up until recently, I could boast of putting four dollars into each bum lamb and selling that same lamb for thirty dollars, which seemed to me to be a good return. Now the lower lamb prices don't make the feeding of higher priced powdered milk replacers, pellets and grain feasible unless a very well-managed operation is maintained.

Inside the sheepshed door is my veterinary shelf containing all the paraphernalia I use in keeping the herd healthy. The shelf holds several hypodermic syringes and bottles of injectable vitamins and antibiotics.

An indispensable item during the calving and lambing season is aminobolic tablets. These tablets contain protein, yeast, amino acids, dextrose and some other goodies which quickly give strength to a weak or chilled animal. For this reason, we call them "pep" pills and I've been tempted more than once to try them myself after seeing what they do for a near-dead lamb!

I always keep a box of baking soda there too. It's good for stomach upsets in lambs. Another handy item is good, old fashioned sourdough stirred right into the lambs' milk. It contains a kind of yeast that aids in healthy digestion.

The most bum lambs I've ever raised at one time was fifty-six; and over the years I've had plenty of time to observe how quickly they form new attachments when taken from their mothers. I know of cases where lambs have died from stress or loneliness, so, whenever possible, I try to leave the little cliques together.

Sometimes a lamb will be too sick or lame to leave the shed to graze, and two or three of his little woolly friends will remain in the shed with him all day and go hungry too. If this isn't true friendship, I don't know what else to call it.

I always choose a bell lamb while the bums are still quite small. I usually pick the dumbest one! I say this because I select the one that is stupid enough to come whenever I call, regardless whether or not I'm going to push pills down their throats or call them across a big ditch full of rushing water. The lambs soon learn to listen for and follow the sound of the bell. This keeps them together better when they're let out to graze.

Many humorous incidents happen around a lambing shed, or maybe we just learn to recognize any bit of levity we can find during the onerous days and nights spent there. Some years we play a radio twenty-four hours a day in the shed, but I've not yet decided whether or not the sheep appreciate it!

Quite often people appear on the scene unexpectedly. They're always amazed at the sight of a gigantic St. Bernard dog walking amicably among the sheep. He isn't a sheep dog and is no help as such; but with his big warm heart, he isn't any problem either, and apparently the sheep know this too. He's usually ignored by us and the sheep alike – with the exception of one day when he got in my way.

I was trying to chase some sheep into the shed, and every time I'd get close to the doorway with them, Boozer, the St. Bernard, would appear in the opening and scare them back. Finally, my temper got the best of me and I shouted some epithet, telling him in no uncertain terms to get out of the door. Imagine my chagrin when a sweet little voice apologized! I whirled in amazement and there stood an elderly little lady just inside the shed. She had come to visit me.

"Mom's over in the sheepshed," is a common refrain during springtime. I've entertained all manner of visitors in the shed, from clergymen, lawyers, insurance men, fund raisers and salesmen to professional rodeo cowboys, a commercial pilot, a paratrooper, teachers, doctors and congressmen. I always suffer a slight shock whenever I'm rocketing about the shed in my patched levis and singing off-key at the top of my lungs, and I hear an affable, "Hello, there!"

Working around sheep is always interesting. Each sheep has a different personality and, in the numerous days of handling and caring for them, you soon learn to recognize many different individuals. Some remind me most vividly of people I know!

Regardless of what a dyed-in-the-wool cattleman will say

about a sheep's grey matter, I firmly believe that a sheep is smarter than a cow any day. A ewe and lamb can recognize each other's blat from a quarter of a mile away. Thus, they can be trailed for long distances without the tedious job of "mothering up".

With cattle, it's a different matter entirely. Sometimes the "mothering-up" process lasts for hours and requires constant alertness on the part of the cowboys to keep the cows and calves from trying to go back to where they last remembered being united.

Another practical feature of a sheep is that it will thrive where a cow would die. A sheep is able to enjoy browsing on weeds, wild rose bushes and other shrubs that a cow wouldn't touch. This is good when a rancher wishes to keep weeds down along ditches and other places without spraying or cutting.

Lambing is much easier now than when I was a youngster. Lacking electricity then, we used lanterns at night for illumination, and hauled water in barrels from the creek. Some sheepmen had power plants installed to pump their water and light their sheds, but we didn't have one. Many were the times that I saw my mother wrap a chilled, half-dead lamb in a gunny sack and lay it on the open door of the wood kitchen range to warm up. Now I just pop any weak lamb under a heat lamp after first poking a "pep" pill down its small throat. Then I go on about my business. Some time later, when I get around to checking on it, the lamb is usually up and looking for a meal.

In the past, I always bought a bottle of cheap whiskey every spring, which I used to stimulate the frail lambs. Quite often my callers helped themselves and became very tipsy before leaving. So, my advice on the subject is – buy a bottle for lambing if you wish. Then give the lambs aminobolic tablets.

The sheepshed at lambing time holds a peculiar kind of fascination for me. There is so much activity going on all the time and so much to watch. I used to sleep, or try to sleep, during my nights in the shed. Usually, I was too cold to sleep. And, just about the time I'd doze off, I'd be awakened by the mutterings and throaty sounds announcing that it was time to go pick up another newborn lamb or two.

Sometimes, several ewes will all lamb together in the same spot and have a general mix-up of lambs. With four ewes, you might have anywhere from four to ten lambs, and none of them are really sure which is their own. Then you have the dubious fun of trying to sort out the pairs and taking any left-overs to the bum lamb pens. When a lamb dies, I "graft" another lamb on the ewe. I simply skin out the dead lamb and tie its "jacket" over the body of a healthy and hungry bum lamb. Usually within a day or two the "jacket" can be removed, as the ewe has accepted the lamb as her own by then.

Our children love to visit the lambing shed and to help out there. When they were very small, I used to keep a high chair there where the current baby could sit and watch the goings-on out of harm's way. Sometimes, I would put the baby into a wash tub (we used them for feeding sheep) and that made a dandy playpen. Usually the children were very good. Only one ever gave me any trouble. He would sneak into the feed supplies and eat the lamb pellets! They did him no damage but I wouldn't recommend them.

Sheep shearing is a craft that few are taking up nowadays. We used to always hire drifters to come and shear, but the problems with their drawing ahead of wages, drinking and

not showing up finally got my husband down. So, with the help of a friend who used to shear sheep, and an old shearing outfit, he started out on three hundred head to learn how for himself.

I think it took us a week, for it was slow going for him as a novice. I tied the fleece as he finished clipping each sheep, and then climbed a ladder to drop the fleece into the tall wool sacks hung from a scaffold. After every few fleeces, I would have to jump down into the sack to "tromp" the wool down firmly. I can't suggest this as a feminine pastime on a hot afternoon! It gets very hot and smelly down in the sack until you've filled it sufficiently to get your head out into the air and, hopefully, into a fresh breeze.

The youngsters played happily about the shed during that long week. They took their afternoon naps snuggled in a quilt on top of an old hayrack.

About all that can be said for shearing is that it's a lot of hard work. The sheep have to be wrangled into the shearing pens where the shearers can grab them easily. The shearer lays hold of a sheep and, by sheer brute force, positions the animal between his knees. The first cut is made between the front legs and down the right side of the belly. The shearer continues on until the entire fleece is removed in one continuous clipping.

When I was a youngster, the shearers used hand blades that looked much like huge scissors, and they received five to fifteen cents per head. Nowadays, the shearers all have electric clippers, and get anywhere from seventy-five cents to a dollar for each sheep sheared.

The wool tier uses a special paper string to tie the fleece after he has rolled it into a compact bundle, flesh side out. Some shearing outfits have hydraulic wool trompers to fill the sacks efficiently, but most people still hire a wool sacker to do the work manually.

I once sheared a sheep by myself. I completed the job, but the poor sheep looked as if it had been plucked instead! Big gobs of wool hung in long tendrils all over it, and the fleece was such a chopped-up mess that I swept the whole thing into the pile of tags! Tags are the little bits of wool or dirty pieces that must be kept separate, and sell for a much lower price.

I love sheep, so I hate to see the big sheep outfits selling off their bands of sheep due to lack of good help and because of the predator problems. Coyotes have become quite numerous again, and lamb seems to be their favorite dish.

One fall, we lost thirty lambs to coyotes. Finally, we began rounding up the herd every night and trailing the sheep in two miles to be locked in the shed overnight. Anyone who has even seen a prime young sheep crippled, down, and half eaten but still alive will not be so quick to take the coyote's part.

Wool has always been an important fiber to man. It's too bad that as people casually select wool clothing or rugs, they do not stop to think of the incredible story that bit of sheep fleece could tell if it were able! Also, lamb is a most excellent meat, highly proclaimed, even by many staunch cattlemen.

As the bumper sticker says, "Ten million coyotes can't be wrong. Eat lamb!"

7

Cooking – Country Style

"She rises while it is still night, and distributes food to her household."
Proverbs 31:15

Anyone who has ever tried to cook breakfast for seven people in the small kitchen of a log house will understand this chapter. And those who haven't might enjoy hearing about it, along with other aspects of ranch cooking. You see, sometimes cooking breakfast was complicated by having as many as three calves and eleven lambs underfoot!

During a cold spring storm, we frequently had to house the baby calves and lambs in the kitchen overnight to keep them from freezing. The animals reclined in front of the combination wood and gas range with an occasional shiver racking their damp bodies. Every now and then, a sorrowful bawl or bleat would announce their hunger pangs. Once dried off and warmed up, they would bump around trying to stand up on the slick linoleum. Their aroma might be labeled "Springtime", but it would never make a big seller.

So, cooking breakfast took on the bizarre appearance of a

new form of hopscotch. I'd have to keep hopping about amongst the sprawled forms trying to turn hotcakes, and standing on one foot to reach the coffee pot. This we all accepted as an integral part of springtime.

Cooking on a ranch is entirely different from cooking as my city friends know it. Here, everything must come in large quantities to satiate the enormous appetites of men doing hard physical labor from dawn until dark. Guests are always welcome on the ranch too. Whoever happens to be around at mealtime is automatically included in the meal. This amounts to many additional people served during the year, so you must always plan ahead to serve lots of extras when figuring out menus.

I can hear my mother's voice plainly stating, "Always serve hot foods *hot* and cold foods *cold*!" This was really a problem in the days before we had electricity, and we didn't have an ice house as some of the neighbors did.

Mom spent long arduous hours over the wood range in the kitchen, even in summer, when it might be ninety degrees in the shade. You can imagine the temperature in the room, especially on canning days, when the huge boilers must be kept boiling for three or four long hours. This required a lot of wood chopping besides.

Keeping the water reservoir at the side of the cookstove filled with water was always my job. There, the water did manage to reach a degree of warmth, and was close at hand when needed.

It really wasn't so hard to cook on the old wood and coal ranges, once you mastered the art of building and keeping a good fire. The huge stove top accommodated a large number of pots and pans. The warming oven above was just right to heat plates, which helped to keep the food warm in the freezing dining room during the meal. It was also an excellent place to raise the bread dough. The large, roomy oven held many loaves of crusty brown bread and was easy to use, once you got the knack of keeping the fire and heat even.

The oven door was a great place to dry out mittens and clothes on a wet rainy day. It was also useful as a footrest when the fire died low. Many are the books I've read by flickering lamplight on a cold winter's night with my feet propped on the warm oven door, letting myself be transported to faraway lands via the printed page.

Serving cold foods cold was the hardest. As a youngster, I must have run many miles to the cellar to fetch the homemade butter before mealtime. It would stay reasonably fresh for a time in the musty dark cool interior of the cellar. I would also like to know how many gallons of water I've pumped at the old fashioned pump in the yard.

Mom would say, "Hurry! The men are coming in for dinner. Pump the water cold for the tea." And pump I would. With brown braids flying and ragged clothes flapping, I worked the old handle fiercely until the well water ran cold into the pitcher for the cold tea. We had no ice in those days.

The garden vegetables were always cleaned outside in a dishpan or washtub. I'm sure, over the years, I've pumped enough water to float a big ship, just washing vegetables.

One thing we missed in the hot summertime was whipped cream. If the kitchen was too hot, as it usually was, the cream wouldn't whip, and ice cream was strictly a wintertime treat. I remember standing at the window, watching my mother run out to a snow bank, uncover a tin syrup pail and stir the contents vigorously before dashing back indoors. During wartime, when sugar was rationed, she made a delicious concoction from cream and honey and froze it in a snowdrift. The frequent stirrings did nothing to smooth out the grainy texture, but we thought it was nectar fit for kings.

I vividly remember my mother getting up before five o'clock in the morning to build up a fire in the cookstove. Then, by the wavering light of a kerosene lamp, she stirred up hotcakes, made coffee, oatmeal and fried meat or eggs. She always cooked a pail of cornmeal mush for the numerous sheep dogs. Then she'd set the table for sometimes up to eight or ten men during the busy seasons.

After breakfast, a large quantity of water had to be heated (this necessitated more wood chopping) to wash the many greasy dishes. By the time this was done it was time to think of dinner. Usually, the bread dough had been set the night before and needed tending in order to have hot fluffy rolls or bread in time for the noon meal.

Then, in cool weather, she would take a large, wicked-looking butcher knife and go outdoors to whack off a piece of meat from the usual mutton or venison hanging from a tree in some shady spot. This carcass was always kept well wrapped in a sheet and a canvas tarp to keep out the flies and magpies.

There was no such thing as a selection of cuts. She merely cut off what she was able to and, if the carcass was frozen, this entailed the use of a meat saw, making the job even more difficult.

During the heat of summer, we had to depend on home canned meat or freshly caught fish from the nearby creek. And, nearly every day, I would get in on the plucking of a few young chickens as Mom needed help in getting them pan-ready in time for meals.

In addition to all this, there was the daily trip to the garden, about a quarter mile away, to bring in the fresh vegetables and salad materials needed for the huge meals. Sometimes, while we were at the garden, we'd hoe a row or two or pick off a pint or two of potato bugs.

So, when I found myself cooking for a six-man haying crew only a few days after I was married, I didn't find it too difficult. I remembered how it used to be and was thankful for the electric stove, the refrigerator and the deepfreeze that we didn't have a few years before.

Instead of a washboard or cranky gasoline engine powered washing machine, I had an electric washer. As a child, I always loved the asthmatic "putt-putt-putt" sound of the old gas Maytag on washday, and I loved the clean smell of the homemade soap we youngsters shaved up into little pieces for Mom. But I didn't miss any of these things at all when I set up housekeeping on my own!

Mom always said the secret of a good meal is to have hot buns just coming out of the oven as the men come in to eat. With that choice fare, they'd never notice if the meat was a bit tough or the pie crust not as flaky as usual. Over the years, I've tried to keep up that practice, and it has led to further experimentation in the field of bread doughs.

We use a lot of sourdough bread here on the ranch, mainly because it does not take the constant watching and punching down that the conventional type of white bread does. It also makes up into fluffy, light, tangy dinner rolls in just one hour. I've seen many a crew turn down pie or cake for dessert in order to have another hot sourdough biscuit with gravy or homemade jam.

In the days when a neighboring rancher hired me to bake for their crew, I used to bake sixteen loaves of bread a week besides the enormous quantities of raised doughnuts, maple sticks, pies and cakes. I won't go further into bread making here. There are many good books on the subject, and everyone develops his or her own little tricks in making good homemade bread. It is sufficient to say that nothing makes a house seem so homey as the smell of fresh bread, and I encourage every young wife to learn how to make it.

On the ranch, we raise a half-acre of vegetables, so there is almost any variety you can wish for from celery to citron. Sometimes we have melons and small sweet potatoes, but usually the harvest in these two items is small. The last year we exhibited at the local fair, we had over seventy entries of all different varieties of vegetables. We were awarded twenty-six blue ribbons and twenty red ones to win the overall sweepstakes in the vegetable department.

It's nice to have this abundance of fresh vegetables for the picking, but you must keep in mind the long hours spent in planting, hoeing, cultivating, irrigating and picking the produce.

When I was small, I helped to cultivate the garden by leading a gentle old work horse up and down between the rows while Mom guided the cultivator behind us. If the flies were not too annoying or it was not too hot, it generally went fairly well. But sometimes the old horse would get cantankerous and deliberately walk down the vegetable rows instead of between them.

My skinny arms were not always strong enough to pull the huge head and Roman nose out of the young corn stalks; so we would wend our way along the rows slowly, with the old horse taking enormous bites every step of the way. I think of this every time I start up my power cultivator and follow it down the neat garden rows.

We always have chickens and sometimes turkeys around, and an occasional pig fattening. It's very convenient to run out and gather a bowlful of fresh eggs whenever you need them, but butchering the young roosters for frying is an unenviable job, especially during fly season.

Company arrives at the ranch nearly every day during the summer months. Our city friends are most envious and full of wistful praise as they sit down to a meal of fried spring chicken, new potatoes, fresh garden salad, perhaps five different vegetables, hot whole wheat buns and a delicate cream pie, smooth with eggs and rich milk.

I've been told that cooking is so easy for country women because they have everything to cook with! Yes, we do. But we also get up about four-thirty every morning to take care of it all! Much of the food for many of our meals is entirely produced or made "from scratch" right here on the home place. To those who argue about the work and trouble involved, I say let's compare flavor and grocery bills!

We have many berries, both wild and tame, so we make up to five gallons of jelly each year. Currants, buffalo berries, rhubarb juice, elderberries, strawberries and wild cherries all make excellent jellies.

We make all of our own hotcake syrup here too, and serve it warm. We started this when our kitchen used to be so cold in wintertime. The kitchen in our log house was the warmest room, and it could only be heated up to a maximum of fifty-five degrees (according to our wall thermometer) during the winter. The water froze on the floor when I tried to scrub it.

We have sourdough hotcakes every morning of the week, except for Sundays. They are easily made because half of the work is accomplished the night before when the batter is set. We make our hotcakes large, dinner plate size, and make extra so that there will be at least ten of them left over for our St. Bernard's breakfast. On a cold day, I dip his in bacon fat or leftover grease for extra nourishment. I solidly believe in the merits of sourdough hotcakes to tide an active man through a cold morning until noontime.

One distinctive feature of sourdough is the fact that it is a very good medicine to take for stomach flu. I first learned this when I read somewhere that missionaries in Africa, lacking sufficient quantities of medicine to treat the natives for dysentery, administered two tablespoons of raw sourdough instead. This they were able to keep in stock as they mixed it in barrels and had only to keep adding flour and milk or water to it in order to make more.

My family and relatives have been using sourdough for several years now to treat upset stomach and flu with great success. Also, I might add that it is supposed to be a great antidote for a hang-over on the morning after!

Now, as I prepare a big meal for a crew of men, I remember not to complain of the extra work and to be thankful instead for the lovely hot water heater and other conveniences. I recall how my mother worked to prepare a meal for twenty threshers all by herself without even running water. The only running water she had when I was a kid was me!

Threshing days were very exciting to us youngsters. The noon meals were huge and the men always rested awhile afterward in the shade of the huge old trees in the yard. All the neighboring men came from miles around with their teams and wagons.

The grain bundles were pitched from their piles (shocks) by hand into the wagons and hauled in alongside the puffing, wheezing threshing machine, where they again were pitched by hand into the machine. The threshing machine was activated by a long flat belt attached to one of the few tractors in the neighborhood. The straw and chaff were blown out into gigantic piles and the grain was run into grain wagons or the pickups of those who had them.

The crews always worked until dark, and I can still remember how exciting it was to stand out in the gathering dusk and watch and listen for the sounds of the men coming in. Sometimes, I could hear the threshing machine shut down if they were in a nearby field. Other times, I'd wait until I heard the sound of the wagons and the jingle of the harnesses before running to tell Mom they were coming.

The horses were always watered and cared for first. Then the men would start straggling toward the house singly or in small groups. They were tired and covered with dust and itchy chaff, but they bantered good-naturedly as they sloshed about, washing up on the bench under a big spreading tree.

The old dining room took on a festive appearance with all the lamps lighted. Long wooden benches were pulled up on each side of the extended table which was covered with two red and white checkered cloths. All the chairs were filled, and I remember one time when we rummaged out two apple boxes to fill in for needed seats. There was always a lot of joking and ribbing at the table as the huge bowls and steaming platters were passed around. The plates were heaped high several times.

I remember that Mom always seemed a bit nervous and preoccupied as she tried to keep the cups and glasses filled. She kept bringing the platters back to the kitchen for refilling with meat and buns. Then it would be my job to carry in the pie plates. I think Mom was always very relieved when threshing was over and all the meals had gone well, even though she was left with a mountain of sticky dishes to wash, the fire to replenish and water to heat.

I recall various times when Mom wished for electricity before we finally got it. Many times at night, before bedtime, she would have liked a cup of coffee, but hated to build up the fire and wait for it. When we finally did get rural electrification in 1949, I was the most excited about having ice cubes, but she always felt it a luxury to be able to make coffee quickly whenever she felt like it.

We used to think and talk a lot about the time when we would be able to have all the conveniences of the city folks. It was always, "maybe next year!"

Now, as I wander down the gleaming, orderly aisles of our supermarket, I see young women filling their carts with prepared mixes and frozen dinners. It's sad to think how many of them depend on others to prepare their meals for them. A lot of young homemakers will never know the satisfaction of putting a good, home-cooked meal on the table for their families.

8

At the Mercy of the Elements

"In the shadow of Your wings I take refuge,
till harm pass by. . ."
Psalm 57:2

The mercury seemed to be frozen at forty degrees below; but, with the fierce winds shaking the old house and rattling the panes, we knew it must equal seventy below with the wind chill factor figured in. Definitely not a nice night, but the kids were sleeping through the storm and we sat up uneasily.

Suddenly a loud thumping and scraping noise on the roof made us leap to our feet. I stood still with heart pounding as John grabbed a flashlight and his parka and raced outside into the black, swirling, blinding snow and death-dealing wind.

When John came in with a blast of frigid air and pushed the kitchen door shut, he stood against it a moment to catch his breath. He looked shaken.

After a bit, he told me the chimney had blown down in the high winds, and what we had heard was the sound of the bricks pelting down on the roof. He said we'd have to let the oil stove go out for he was afraid the flying sparks might ignite our old wooden shingles. He had no way of fully assessing the damage in the darkness, but he thought our chimney had been torn off flush with the house. For heat, we would have to depend only on a wood fire in the kitchen range which had a separate chimney, and it was a large and drafty old house.

Without a word, I went into the pantry and selected a few items which I laid out on the kitchen table within easy reach – some canned meat, bread and coffee. Quietly we agreed that, if the house caught on fire, John would grab up the two sleeping children and I would take the food and some blankets. We would seek shelter in the bunkhouse where we could build a fire in the wood heater to keep from freezing to death.

There was no use trying to get help. The phone was out; the power might go any minute if the lines went down, as they frequently did during a severe storm. Our nearest neighbors were over three miles away and the roads were blocked. Even with our four-wheel drive vehicle, it would be sheer madness to try to get out over the ridges on a night like this. Our best bet was to stay put.

We got into bed with the sleeping kids for warmth, and spent the rest of the stormy night wide awake, listening and smelling for smoke. The house cooled off rapidly and the water pipes froze. The long hours before the January dawn came were torturous ones, for we both feared that we'd lose stock in the storm but we didn't speak of it.

Morning came at last and, with tired, red-rimmed eyes, we looked out at a white world filled with monstrous snowdrifts, but many of the ridges and mountainsides were swept bare. The wind had died down. It was still forty below; and in the pink dawn, the mountain peaks gleamed with a stately majesty that never failed to give me a lonesome feeling deep inside.

Our sheep had drifted several miles, but luckily had not been snowed under and buried alive as we first suspected. We lost no cattle, but slowly reports trickled in of the terrible losses to the east of us where there was less shelter. Some ranchers lost up to fifty head of cattle, and one friend of ours suffered such loss that he went out of the cattle business.

This was only one of many winter storms. Montana weather can be devastating. One night, though it was only twenty below, the wind was so severe we lost five calves in a twelve hour period. They simply froze to death as soon as they were born. Many times, the livestock will seek shelter, only to become buried alive when the snow drifts in over the top of them and they are unable to get out.

Sometimes, during a heavy, wet spring snowstorm, we would have to take shovels and scoop the weighty mass off the roofs of sheepsheds or other flat buildings to keep the timbers from breaking under the weight.

Feeding the livestock during the winter was frequently anything but fun. John used to have to make a twelve mile

circuit with a team of horses and bobsled to distribute feed to all the livestock. He always came back tired and hungry and, if it was very cold, he would have frozen his face.

I recall one winter when he was breaking a new horse to work. It was a terribly nerve-wracking time for me. One day the team came running by the house, dragging the broken sled tongue. They were white with lather and steaming in the cold from a long hard run as they pounded by me in the direction of the barn. I knew there had been an accident. John could be injured and unable to reach home, and might freeze to death, but there was nothing I could do.

Our phone was dead again and I was a prisoner in the house with two tiny girls. The wind had come up and the drifting snow would have obliterated any tracks the team had made. The visibility lessened, and it grew colder and colder. I waited in an agony of worry for nearly an hour before John came walking in through the knee-deep snow. I was weak with relief.

The next day was a repeat performance of the day before; but this time, John wisely tied his saddle horse to the back of the sled, so he came riding in shortly on the heels of the runaway team. Eventually, he did get the team lined out to work fairly well, but many times he had to actually shovel them out when they mired down in the belly-deep snowdrifts and were unable to move. Oh, the life of a real cowboy isn't nearly so glamorous as it appears on television!

During one night of fifty-six degree below weather, our heating stove went out. We were living in a log house at the time and heating with propane. The propane got so cold it wouldn't flow through the pipe and the stove went out.

John quickly dressed and went outside into the severe winds. He used a portable hand torch to warm up the big propane tank until it would again vaporize and flow so that the stove would burn. It took nearly an hour, altogether. During this time I kept stoking the wood stove in the kitchen. But, in spite of my efforts, the temperature plummeted to thirty degrees inside the house before we were able to get the heater going again. And John again frosted his face and hands while working out in the bitter night to heat up the tank.

It was hard to raise babies in such cold old houses. They always had to be bundled up, almost as though they were going outside. They couldn't play on the drafty floors either; and baths were quickly given in front of the open oven door, with the clothing draped nearby to warm up.

At night, the present baby was always put to bed right in front of the heating stove. Many were the nights that one of us had to get up and move a cold and crying baby closer to the heat. If the baby rolled over to the far side of the crib, it soon became cold and woke up. I finally resorted to using big safety pins to pin the infant's pajamas to the mattress and thus keep it nearer to the heat.

Once, during a rigorous cold spell, I developed a severe case of pneumonia. I had medicine from the doctor, and he had strictly ordered me to stay in bed and drink lots of fluids. I filled a large glass with water and, placing it on the bedside table, I sank into a deep feverish slumber. Awhile later, when I awakened and reached over for a drink, imagine my consternation when I discovered the water in the glass had frozen solid!

During the winter, I expected to be snowed-in, but the longest I was ever housebound was two months at one time. John, of course, was able to bundle up and get out. Sometimes he got only as far as the neighbors, three and a half miles away, to pick up the mail on horseback; but I was stuck at home with the children.

However, I don't recall ever being bored because I liked to read and did a lot of sewing. We always kept a big supply of groceries on hand, and the long winters gave me ample time to experiment with new recipes.

I do recall a terrible craving for fresh oranges one time. We had fruit, but it was all home-canned and I wanted oranges so desperately that I even dreamed repeatedly of them. Once I woke up and believed that I could actually smell them! When John was finally able to get to town, you can bet oranges were on my list in big letters and, ironically enough, he forgot to get them! I shed a few tears in private, then went on thinking and tasting oranges for nearly a month before I got any. It was really a dream come true when I finally got my long-sought oranges. I ate three all at once.

Probably one of the most horrifying and depressing sights I've ever seen in ranching was the time I saw a fortune lost in a mid-May snowstorm. A neighbor had sheared his herd of yearling ewes and had just turned down a big offer for the entire herd. No sooner had he turned the sheep out to graze on the new green grass when a late storm hit unexpectedly.

After the storm passed over, I saw a thousand head of sheep lying dead over a widely scattered area of the mountains. In one place, the carcasses were piled so high they actually dammed the mountain stream with their bodies. Some died on their feet; others were in small bunches where they had tried to seek shelter under overhanging ledges and trees. Twisted shapes were laying everywhere I looked.

This man was a rancher who loved sheep, and he had been deeply hurt. But rather than embarrass others, and not wanting their pity, he smiled broadly when he said, "Well, this is the biggest loss I've ever had yet. One year I lost ten thousand dollars on a bunch of calves. This sure beats that all to blazes!"

This is one reason why my feelings are so profound for the stockman. He stands like a young willow, ready to spring back with a snap after experiencing some unbelievable setbacks.

The first winter after my marriage, we worked for the P Cross Ranch, a very old and famous ranch south of Havre. John and the foreman used teams and sleds to feed hay to the cattle, but every day they also hauled a heavy wagonload of grain to about four hundred head of cattle. This necessitated the use of two teams, due to the heavy weight of the grain.

It was a thrilling sight to watch the four big work horses straining at the tugs and kicking up snow as they faithfully delivered grain to the livestock. Seldom did anyone around there ever work four horses at that time.

Winters aren't the only hard times on a ranch. I've seen seven inches of rain fall within half an hour. The deluge came so fast that the drought-hardened soil couldn't absorb it, and it ran off, forming huge rivers that washed out stretches of fence, posts and all, for over half a mile. In other places, the rushing torrent washed giant holes in the ground twelve feet deep.

One such storm drove a large number of our cattle into the corner of a new and tight fence. Fortunately, the calves were able to escape through the taut wires, but three of the older cows were trampled to death and buried under two feet of mud and manure churned up in the corner. It was a heart-sickening sight, and so were the little calves, all plastered with mud and dung.

Another time, we had a similar cloudburst in the middle of the night. The rain washed down from the mountains in waves, down the coulee to our house and right into the outside doorway of our basement. It might not have been so bad, except that we had just planted a new lawn and covered it with straw. The basement was filled with six inches of water, mud and straw. We used scoop shovels and wash tubs to scrape up the mass and carry it out, as the floor drain had become clogged with debris.

Hail is a very real threat during the hot summer months. Many times a rancher has a fine stand of hay or grain ready to cut, only to lose it all within minutes during a savage hailstorm.

Last summer, close friends of ours lost all their grain and half of their hay crop. They lost many thousands of dollars in the fields, not to mention the cost of reroofing their buildings and replacing window glass. It was a savage storm that covered a path more than twenty miles long and several miles wide.

Every coulee and depression ran with several feet of water; and the angry waters lashed out in fury to wipe out roads, fences and many bridges. The leafless trees and bushes lifted scraggly limbs skyward in the wake of the storm, looking much like any fall scene. Even the tough old sagebrush had been stripped of its leaves.

The morning after this costly storm, we went to visit our good friends to see how they were taking it. I was heartsick to see that what had once been a fine garden now looked like a plowed field with gullies washed down the middle of it. Everywhere lay wreckage and debris from the storm.

I approached the house with trepidation, wondering just how to offer my condolences, when the door was thrown open and we were greeted warmly with big smiles. Over coffee, they joked about their loss and not having to do any haying. But throughout the conversation, the theme of "next year, things will be better" kept threading its way.

Lightning storms in Montana are to be feared by all, especially when the grass is tinder-dry and the timber smells as if it is ready to explode.

In the mountains, we sometimes had terrible lightning storms nightly, when the crackling, snapping electricity set fire to haystacks and sent giant pines crashing to the ground. It was always a relief to hear the patter of rain on the roof and know that the danger of fire had diminished.

One summer I spent alone in the mountains with our then two very small girls. The elevation at my house was forty-eight hundred feet, but the surrounding peaks towered to over five thousand. I was the only one living in that particular area for many square miles.

I spent my nights pacing the floor from window to window, watching the sky while the lightning lit up the heavens and thunder shook the very foundation and rattled the dishes in my kitchen. It was a very dry summer. Without rain, the nightly fire danger increased. Finally, lightning did start several bad fires; but, thanks to the quick help of many ranchers from miles around, they were extinguished before burning more than a few hundred acres.

Another time when I was all alone with the children, a bolt of lightning came through the window. It looked exactly like a large, sparkling tumbleweed. It rolled about the house for a few minutes, giving the youngsters and me a terrible fright before vanishing into an electrical outlet.

Our neighbors weren't so fortunate when a bolt came into their house. It burned a large hole in the wall of their kitchen.

An amusing side to the terrifying storms was the fact that, after a really bad lightning storm, the lightning rod salesmen were sure to be out in full force the next day! They usually found a fertile field, and lightning arresters bristled from everyone's sheds and outbuildings!

No matter how frightening a lightning storm can get, I always find something awesome about it too. Man has control over so many things, but lightning has the power to make the bravest man cower in his heart. I like to think that it's God shoving things around and making a lot of racket just to remind man of his infinitesimal existence and his dependence on the Creator. Also, He is very generous with the nitrogen during these storms which really gives the crops a boost.

Whenever I see a cow struck dead by lightning, it makes me wonder why that particular cow was selected from amidst the herd. Sometimes cattle will crowd together in a fence corner during a storm, and lightning will come along the fence wires and kill the whole bunch. I always wonder what makes one post in a long row so vulnerable. While the others go unscathed, it lays in splinters from a strike. To me, it is this sense of insecurity and uncertainty that makes the lightning so intimidating.

On one occasion, we happened to be driving cattle on the prairie near the Canadian border when a devastating storm broke loose abruptly. The nearest building or shelter of any kind was miles away, so we simply kept going. The bolts of lightning were striking the prairie all around us and, at each close one, my saddle horse would slide to a trembling halt and stand still with legs splayed out, nostrils flaring and eyes rolling. You could feel the electricity in the air as sparks danced and jumped about the horses and their bridles. Regardless of all we had learned about horses being good attractors of electricity, we still did not dismount and lay on the ground.

We shouted to each other to be heard over the roar of the

storm, and then beat it on a dead run for the ranch buildings several miles away. That day, I truly thought I was going to meet my Maker and I was prepared to die. But we made it safely with only a good soaking and a healthy respect for lightning storms on the wide open prairie.

Drought can be a great anxiety when your livelihood depends on the revitalizing effects of a slow, soaking rain. After the toils, lack of sleep and frustrations encountered in ranching and farming, it is most heartbreaking to see it all come to an untimely end for lack of rain.

You drive out to check the cattle and notice anxiously how the water holes shrink daily and springs dry up. The grass becomes brittle and powder dry so that even the cattle walking around shatters it. You watch the hot winds swirl the dust and wonder how many calves will succumb to dust pneumonia.

You're sorry to hear that some of your friends have to haul water to their herds and are driving over a hundred miles a day to do so. Still others are suffering death loss from having cattle drink the putrid mud in the drying water holes. Many have to market early because their grass dried up completely; and the selling weights of the cattle were most disappointing, to say the least.

Every day you watch the sky, and each little gathering of clouds fills you with new hope. Then they either dissipate or you live through another night of wicked dry lightning. In the morning, the white-hot sun beats down unmercifully, again causing great cracks and fissures in the parched earth. The grain curls up and turns from its former lusty green to a terminal yellow. The grass is bleached white. The dusty trees droop beneath the daily scorching, and evergreens smell for miles.

We've seen some bad years of continued drought, but nothing compared to those my mother lived through in the early 1900's. At that time, her creek dried up completely, something it hasn't done since, and only a few scummy water holes remained at scattered intervals where a few dependable springs held out. Neighbors from miles away came daily with lumber wagons and teams to fill their barrels with the precious liquid and then headed back to their homes. One rancher sold off all of his herd except for fifteen head of cows, and then had to buy hay to feed even that few through the winter. There was absolutely no grass at all for grazing.

If the hail, floods, bad winters, lightning and drought don't wipe you out, then the bugs might. Grasshoppers come in droves some years and leave a path of destruction behind them equal to a bad hailstorm. When I was a baby, a type of cricket that was locally called "Morman Beetle" became so numerous that the men dug trenches around the fields, poured poison into them and killed many off that way.

Despite all the hearbreaks and financial setbacks, the western stockman and farmer holds out bravely, consoling himself with the thought that, surely, "things will be better next year!"

9

Cowboys and Other Critters

"You are the salt of the earth. . ."
Matthew 5:13

Twilight was deepening into night as the two cowboys approached the darkened house. They had watched the occupants leave, but still they proceeded slowly lest they were mistaken in their belief that no one was at home.

Once they were assured that they were alone, they proceeded gleefully with the task they had assigned themselves.

Outside the house stood a huge stack of cement blocks left over from some construction job. These they lugged into the house with alacrity. Their attention centered first on the bedroom. Together, they were able to maneuver the heavy blocks under the bed; and they kept adding to the growing pile until the bed was raised to an alarming height.

Next, they moved into the kitchen, which was the first room of the house to be entered. Since the light switch was some distance from the door, they built a barricade of cement blocks about shin-high, just where a person coming home in the dark would be most likely to hit it. Then, with a blithe sense of accomplishment, they quietly left.

Would you believe these were all good friends? Yes, they were, but they were cowboys. And a cowboy likes nothing better than to play tricks on his friends. Usually, everything is taken in the spirit of fun; and, strangely enough, no one ever seems to get hurt, which is surprising, considering that some of the ploys are sometimes dangerous. Other times, they prove to be a bit costly.

A young man we knew got married. You can always tell how well-liked a man is by the amount of trouble his compatriots rain upon him. If his wedding comes off unmarred, you can bet he isn't more than a casual friend to the other cowboys.

Anyhow, this certain young man brought his bride home to his modest ranch house and proceeded to build up a lively fire in the wood stove. Soon they were coughing and choking in the billows of dense smoke that engulfed them as they fled the house. He was able to spot the trouble when he climbed up to the roof and removed the two good feather pillows that his "friends" had stuffed into the chimney.

He had occasion to learn later that his friends had also smeared honey all over the toilet seat in the outdoor privy! This man was liked by all. But he had done more than his share of harassment to others, so he was only getting it back.

Another popular trick was for a couple of guys to hide under the bed in a newlyweds' house. They generally gave themselves away by not being able to remain silent. Usually, they had imbibed too much and tended to look upon everything with exaggerated hilarity.

Once, a handsome young cowboy came courting my older sister. He was all slicked up to make a good impression and was riding a fine looking animal which he tied to our yard fence. He then proceeded to devote the entire evening, until quite late, to the object of his affections. He was doing just fine too, until it was time for him to go out, mount his spirited horse and make an impressive departure in the moonlight.

You can imagine his shock, and then his humiliation, at finding his horse gone! The bridle was still tied to the post, so he assumed that his horse had managed to rub it off and go on home alone. Due to the lateness of the hour and to the distance away that he lived, he was further embarrassed by having to ask someone to take him home.

When he arrived home and went to the barn, he was amazed to find his horse tied in its stall, fed and with the saddle removed. His good friends had played a mean trick on him by stealing his horse, but they had taken pains to see that the horse received proper treatment!

An old trick that cowboys like to play on any "dude" coming into the area is the "snipe hunt." The dude is taken far away from any ranch buildings to a secluded spot and left to hold a gunny sack and a lantern while the others go off to chase the snipes down the coulee and into his waiting bag. They go off and literally leave him holding the bag! Some hours later, when he discovers that he has been duped and walks the long way home, he is received royally. If he takes it all with good-natured grace, chances are he won't remain a tenderfoot much longer.

One bachelor cowboy I know often had to cook for the many men whom he had asked to help him. He told me he intended to put green food coloring into the hotcake batter when he fixed breakfast for the riders. Then he would make some suitable comments about the appearance of the eggs he had used in the batter when he set the hotcakes on the table.

I never heard if he actually went ahead with it, but I

suggested to him that he put Ex-Lax in the next chocolate pie he made for company if he really wished to put the "run" on them.

I doubt if he actually did that either, as the guy was most hospitable and welcomed anyone to his home. The only thing he ever asked was that anyone who stayed overnight take off his overshoes before getting into bed!

Recently, a well-known and admired rancher was hospitalized with something or other that was not too serious. However, his large host of friends got together and all sent him get well cards, but they purposely neglected to put any stamps on them. So, while the recuperating man was delighted by the heavy deluge of mail, he was also overwhelmed by the amount of the postage due!

I know a family of rugged cowboys who used to ranch beside a big river. They carried water from the river uphill to their log house some distance away. The water was used for all household needs including drinking, and they never suffered any ill effects.

One day a party of fishermen stopped by and one of the women walked the trail up to the house to ask for a drink of decent water. She said that she absolutely couldn't stomach the thought of drinking that filthy river water. With straight faces, they served her a dipper of water and she went away grateful for the good drink, never knowing that she had drunk river water after all and had walked uphill to do so.

I've often heard the following story and believe it to be true. A rancher found an old neighbor dead in an isolated shack. Since it was winter, the body was frozen stiff. So, without ceremony, the rancher loaded the corpse into the back of his big old car and set out for town with it. The roads were bad and the big car had a tough time making it through all the chuck holes and snowdrifts. Consequently, the dead man did a lot of lurching about in the back seat.

As the rancher was going along at a good clip, plowing through the snow, he was hailed by a neighbor along the road and slammed on his brakes. When he did so, the body in the back seat tumbled forward into the front. Calmly, the rancher extended an arm and pushed the body back into position again with a, "Will you *please* stay in the back?" The neighbor along the road stood dumbfounded, which was just what the rancher had hoped for.

My Grandpa was a tough old settler who would work like the devil was after him, and then take a few days off and liven up the burgeoning town of Havre. He always included his pistol in any fun that he had; and, after he had shot up a saloon or two, he would go home to work hard for another six months or a year. Whenever Grandpa got out his jug and

his pistol, everyone ran for cover. He was fond of making lots of racket and enjoyed the sound of the pistol firing. Then Grandma would sneak out and either break his jugs on the rocks or empty them to shorten the duration of his spree.

My Grandma Kearful was a rather intrepid individual herself. She was the one who usually went into town to market the produce from their many gardens, and she frequently carried large sums of cash around with her. It was no secret. Grandpa was known as the "Cabbage King" around Havre in the early 1900's, and Grandma was well-known too.

My mother has frequently recounted this experience to me. Grandma and my mother, who was then only ten years old, had completed their selling early in Havre, and had started out on the eighteen mile trip to their homestead. Grandma was a very accomplished horsewoman and always drove or rode the best to be had. They were jouncing along on the high spring seat of the lumber wagon, enjoying the beautiful day and the fine sense of achievement in a job well done, when two men jumped out from cover. The men came out on opposite sides of the road and each one grabbed for the head of a horse.

"Get down on the floor, Marion!" Grandma commanded the frightened, skinny child clinging to the high seat beside her. Then Grandma snatched the buggy whip from its socket and firmly planted her sturdy shoes on the dashboard. That lively team had never before felt the touch of a whip and when she laid it on them, they lunged forward in wild panic. They rocketed up the trail, leaving two surprised would-be robbers lying in a swirl of dust on the road. Grandma kept the team running until she had covered a safe distance and then resumed her deliberate way homeward.

Although Grandma was not easily frightened by man or beast, Mom remembered how she practiced with a pistol for several days after that incident. Also, Grandpa made a leather holster which he attached to the wagon seat. Grandma never went to town after that without her pistol, which she discreetly covered with a lap robe.

Orrie "Kid" Tibbets was an old-time cowboy and rancher in Blaine County who was well-known to all. He was my great uncle.

Kid Tibbets came to Montana from Illinois about 1889. He arrived in the fall with his sixteen-year-old sister, Flora, who later became my grandmother. Accompanying them were two elderly aunts who had raised them. What makes the story unusual is the fact that Kid was only fourteen at the time.

They arrived in the late fall with little time to prepare for the severe Montana winter. But despite his lack of years, Kid Tibbets was a man, and his resourcefulness brought them safely through the winter. The family lived in a sod house with a dirt floor during that first winter; but Kid tied in with a will, and they were prepared by the time the next winter rolled around.

Tibbets was very talented as an artist, and he taught himself to write with a very flowery script which, I'm sure, in earlier times would have won him great recognition as a "scribe." He was a self-educated man like countless others were in those days.

Later, his wandering nature and restless drive made him sell out his fine ranch on Clear Creek and move to Canada. By this time, his sister had long been married to Jerry Kearful and the aunts had passed on.

At first, Kid bought a ranch in Canada just across the border from Montana, but that couldn't hold him either. He moved to British Columbia and purchased a large portion of a place called Lulu Island. Although I was only five when I

visited there, I shall never forget the beauty of the towering pines, the fruit trees, the majestic mountains, the roaring ocean and the sound of fog horns in the harbor.

I believe Kid Tibbets was happy on Lulu Island. He started a chicken business and opened a grocery store. He owned rental property, but his big thing was a newspaper he started. There, he finally found the outlet for his creative talents and his moving energies. He passed away there about 1945 after leading a full and varied life.

My father-in-law told me of a time when he was a young lad, and he and a bunch of young folks decided to go to a dance twenty miles over the mountains. The team they used was a pair they were only just beginning to break to drive and was very hard to manage. So, whenever a gate loomed on the scene, someone was obliged to jump out and run to open it.

Then they would drive the team in circles until that fellow could close the gate, catch up and jump in.

I think stockmen are the grandest people on earth. Their affinity with nature and animals makes them very sensitive to the needs of their fellow man.

I liked what one old weather-beaten cowboy told me one time. He said he didn't feel the need to go to church on Sundays as I did. He said, "I don't have to sit in a building with lots of duded-up folks to find God!" He told me he felt God was all around him; and the mountains and the skies were his cathedral, where he could worship God within sight of His mighty handiwork.

Once, when my husband was sick in bed with mumps complicated by flu, a very good neighbor rode over every day the three and one-half miles to feed our cattle. It was a tough winter and we were short on hay; but we had purchased a large quantity of rolled barley which we fed on the ground to the cattle. I sacked up the grain each morning, and this fine gentleman would ride in, harness our team and hook them up to the sled, load the sacks and we were off.

Sometimes I rode along on a saddlehorse to round up the cattle that were scattered over the hills rustling (looking for grass). Some days, when the wind was really strong, the cattle would never leave the sheltering timber at all, and we were obliged to carry the sacked grain back into the trees to feed them.

All this took quite some time, and I remember one day being concerned for my husband and the two little tots at the house. I asked this kind friend what time we would get back. I remember how he squinted up at the sun and then looked at me before asking, "What's the difference? We ain't goin' back 'til we're done."

When I questioned him again, he gave me an estimate of

four o'clock in the afternoon. Now, this man had never carried a watch in his life. His wife had once presented him with one, but he lost it a few days later when he was shipping cattle. He had never owned another one since. But, knowing this man well, I didn't think to question his judgment, and wasn't at all surprised to walk into my kitchen later on and see the time on the wall clock was consistent with his earlier estimate.

Once, a mean cow hit me and pinned my wrist in the barn door. I was sure it was broken, but this same neighbor said no, and bandaged it up for me with strips of an old cotton sheet. It was well again in about a week. This was while John was still sick in bed, and I hated to ask any of our neighbors to "dig out" and take me the forty-eight miles to a doctor. I was most thankful for this knowledgeable friend's assistance.

During the sixteen years that I've known him, this same rancher has been a great inspiration to me. Always kind, always gentle, never hurrying – yet he is capable of doing anything. He is an excellent cook, and it was he who taught John how to shear sheep.

He and his gracious wife live in a very relaxing, friendly home that was once part of the original log house on the ranch and was later remodeled. They are surrounded by geese, ducks, turkeys, peacocks and fowls of a variety to match a small zoo. They maintain a large yard with an astounding assortment of flowers and a most complete vegetable garden. They have a greenhouse which enables them to raise all their own plants, and keeps their house filled with many rare and exotic houseplants.

This man's talents defy description. He is an expert butcher, taxidermist, carpenter, plumber, electrician and television and radio repairman. He fixes appliances, and his skill as a doctor or veterinarian is well-known over a wide area.

In fact, I've found nothing that he couldn't do and do well. This even includes fishing, hunting, bowling, horseshoe pitching and card playing. Children just naturally gravitate toward him and, while he sits calmly visiting, there is usually a flock of them hanging onto him or perched on his lap.

This remarkable man once told me that a person should try to learn to do everything he possibly could in this world. I never forgot it, and I've tried to follow his advice. One day he drove in and was visibly amazed to find me with tractor and blade, digging a hole in the ground where we intended to build a greenhouse.

I know a very nice lady who was, and probably still is, as good a ranchhand as lots of young men. During the early years of marriage, she sometimes lived with her husband in a tent while he was busy with his numerous traplines.

The one thing she really desired was to own a washing machine. Her family was growing and she really needed one. So this resourceful gal hired herself a babysitter and went out trapping coyotes on her own, fortified with nothing but her determination. Before long, she had made enough money from the bounty paid on the coyotes she'd trapped to more than pay the babysitter and buy the washing machine. Today, this woman is a grandmother, but she still helps her husband on the traplines. She does some of the skinning yet, which takes skill and experience if you wish to command a high price for your furs.

Stockmen and cowboys are some of the most comfortable people to be with; some of the greatest people on earth, I believe. I could fill a whole volume of stories about real-life cowboys, instead of just this one chapter. Their tales of intrepidity and feats of courage and endurance are unbeliev-able unless you understand this breed of men. Their kind belong in a class of their own, for it was their kind who opened up the frontiers and made them safe for settlement.

I know of some cowboys who kill many rattlesnakes each year, simply by stomping on their heads with the heel of a riding boot. I've seen others kill them by picking up the reptile by its tail and swinging it overhead with a snap that breaks the snake's neck. I wouldn't try either method and wouldn't advise anyone else to either!

I once watched in terrified helplessness as a handsome young bronc rider was dragged for what seemed like hours, but in reality it was only minutes. His boot had hung up in the stirrup when he was thrown from the horse. In horror, I saw the slim athletic body being kicked and trampled by the bronc's pounding hoofs.

The young man did survive. However, he was unconscious for several weeks and hospitalized for many more. I believe only a rough and tough cowboy in top form could have recovered from such an ordeal.

I guess you might say the only thing I really like about cows is the cowboys!

10

Beef and More Bull

"The just man takes care of his beast. . ."
Proverbs 12:10

The deep, dark night was bitterly cold. Curtains of stinging sleet were knifing down, driven by the raging wind from the savage heart of the storm. The tough and bitter thrust of winter had hit us just at calving time.

This night, John had to get up every three hours to check the cattle. Any calf born would soon freeze to death unless sheltered, and our cattle were ranging loose in a three hundred acre calving field with only brush for shelter.

Our reliable old four-wheel drive pickup chewed through the drifted snow and freezing mud holes as John used his searchlight to ferret out the cattle hiding in the brush. They stood humpbacked to the wind, white with a coating of frozen rime. The cattle swung their heads about to face the invading light, but didn't move from their sheltering locations. Anyway, they were getting used to the blinding illumination every few hours.

John had fashioned a searchlight from an airplane landing light and wired it into his pickup. It was much more brilliant and penetrating than the usual spotlight.

The silvery pellets coming against the headlights looked like a shower of sparks, making John slightly dizzy. Suddenly, he was aware of another light nearby. It was a vehicle with a spotlight trying to focus on him.

John wondered who could be out on such a night, trying to follow him around with a spotlight. It must be a neighbor, he decided, wanting help with a heifer calving. He turned slowly in a wide arc beside the brush, checking cattle as he drove along. The meandering line of brush would eventually take him back to where the approaching lights were. There had been a cow back in here acting "calfy" on his last inspection trip, so he went on. However, he did notice that the lights had stopped and then were diffusing wildly as the driver tried to rock his vehicle out of the frozen slough he had inadvertently driven into.

John finished his circle of the field and advanced on the strange vehicle. It had managed to get out of the mud, but was sitting strangely still, stabbing the night with its spotlight, trying to pinpoint John.

When John pulled up alongside the visitor, the driver had his window rolled down and queried vehemently, "What in the blazes do you think you're doing?"

Puzzled, my husband shifted his tobacco before answering mildly, "I'm checking my cows."

"Oh."

The young brand inspector was deflated. He had been working long hours in an attempt to stop the thieving of baby calves that were then bringing the rustlers up to a hundred and thirty dollars apiece. He had been patrolling our county road, looking for anything suspicious; and he had thought he was really on the trail of something hot. All he had gotten, in his eagerness, was "stuck." After a few brief words, he left to continue his lonely vigil on the back roads, looking for calf thieves.

During calving time, most of the ranchers I know make the threat of selling out. They become bleary-eyed with lack of sleep and frustrated with the weather and the cattle themselves. Some days, they'd like to give the place away – anything – just to get some sleep. But as soon as things get straightened out and the weather warms up, they get some sleep. Then they wouldn't dream of doing anything else.

Calving time is one of the busiest times of the year for the rancher. The two-year-old heifers having their first calf must be watched closely, as they often have difficulty giving birth. If the calf is coming in the right position, it can usually be "pulled" with a special device known as a calf puller. If it is not in the right position or is too large, a Caesarean section must be performed. If the animal can be loaded into a horse trailer and taken to the veterinary hospital, the task is much easier. The vets are all overworked, so we usually try to take the animal to them whenever possible, rather than demanding that they come to the ranch.

"Watching heifers" seems to be a wife's job in the spring. It isn't so bad if your husband or a hired man is on the place to call in times of trouble; but it can be terribly nerve-wracking when you're alone and need help, and all the neighbors are either also gone or not answering their phones.

Some of the calves surviving a difficult delivery are quite stupid and need much coaxing to suck. Sometimes it is quite awhile before they learn to suck on their own. This involves much work for the tired rancher, who must either suckle the calf or pour milk into it with a stomach tube.

Next comes a bright day on a snowfall, and you have sunburned udders if you're raising Hereford cattle, as we do. This can be much work, for the cows will not allow the calves to suck. Therefore, they must be run into a chute, milked out and greased up with soothing ointment. Occasionally, a cow will be hobbled with a burlap sack and turned back out with her calf. The sack finally rots or falls off; but by then, her udder is healed up sufficiently for the calf to nurse.

Branding day is an annual highlight for all the youngsters. We always have plenty of help, but the kids like nothing better than to pitch in and wrestle the calves. Two calf wrestlers hold the calves down while someone burns the brand on with a hot iron. The calf is also earmarked, castrated if necessary, vaccinated, and a dehorning paste is applied at this time. If we're branding late in the season, we have ropers on horses to "heel" the calves and drag them up close to the branding fire for the wrestlers. Otherwise, the baby calves are simply penned in a small area and the wrestlers catch and throw them by hand.

After branding comes all the sorting and trailing of cattle to go out onto the different ranges. Every time we're working cattle, we always ask the help of "Top Hand." He's a good friend and an excellent hand with horses and cattle. Top Hand belongs to the old vanishing breed of cowmen – a bit crusty, but with a heart of gold. He'll drink anything. He's not particular, as long as it pours. His speech can only be labeled as X-rated, but even the old ladies flutter when he tips his hat to them on the street.

I've seen Top Hand "top" off a horse on a cold frosty morning and never even lose the cigarette out of his lips. One time he was thrown unexpectedly when his bronc exploded seven miles from home. He bit the dirt, but never lost hold of

the reins. After he had remounted, he smiled easily and said that one thing he'd learned at an early age was never to lose his reins when he got thrown. He didn't like walking that well.

Another time John and our kids were helping Top Hand move his own cattle on a twenty-five mile drive when they stopped for supper in a sheltered coulee to let the cattle graze and rest for the night. After eating, everyone began gathering up the lunch mess to put away. But Top Hand, in his usual high humor, stood in the back of the pickup and began tossing the paper plates and other garbage to the four winds. When reprimanded by the crew, he smiled his secret smile and said, "Heck, it'll all be gone by morning!"

And it was too. However, early the next morning, when

the riders arrived at daybreak to continue the drive, the first sight that greeted their eyes was an old cow walking around with a twisted beer can caught in her front hoof! The riders responded with their usual good-hearted ribbing, which Top Hand can take or dish out equally well.

Although he's always the life of the party, keeping everyone in good humor, no matter how trying the circumstances can get, he is also a tough character to cross. Maybe this goes back to the days when he served with the military police overseas.

Several years ago, the local law officers drove into his yard and informed him to be on the alert for a jailbreaker known to have fled to that particular area.

Not one to get excited, Top Hand said he'd keep a "look out" for the man.

A short time later, he noticed his cattle running around in the calving field some distance from the house. He knew something had excited them, so he took his pickup and went to look. Although he drove around for some time, he was unable to spot anything in all the dense undergrowth. He returned to the ranch buildings, saddled his horse and, taking a pistol, he again set off back to the cattle. He could tell by their actions that they were uneasily watching something foreign in the brush.

While Top Hand was out beating the brush, so to speak, his good wife was anxiously watching from the upstairs windows for what seemed like ages before he came into sight.

He was riding leisurely along with his pistol held carelessly before him. In front walked the jailbreaker. The procession made its way slowly to the house, where he casually told his wife to call the law, seated the wanted man in the yard, and then nonchalantly went into his shop to work on something he was overhauling. He never mentioned this incident, and I found out about it quite by accident. For Top Hand, it was all in a day's ride.

During the summer months, while the calves and yearlings are growing fat and ready for market, they still must be watched for pinkeye, hoof rot and other diseases. Sometimes this involves roping the animal on the range and doctoring it right there on the spot.

John has a faithful old cowhorse, Roany, now retired, that has helped him to doctor untold numbers of cattle. That horse could think like a man. When John would rope a bull in the timber, Roany would quickly look for a tree to brace himself against, as he knew he couldn't hold a full-grown bull.

Once John roped a bull in a rather barren draw. Old Roany did his best to stop the bull, but it was a losing battle and he was sliding along with feet braced. When they finally came upon some brush, Roany was quick to take advantage of a scrubby little willow. By the time I caught up to them, they had the bull at a standstill, but the willow had been pulled up and was leaning across Roany's back. All I could see of him was his powerfully muscled rump and his wise old head sticking out of the green, leafy mass. These good cowhorses are invaluable to their owners.

Trailing cattle in the fall is another big event. Times were when everyone trailed to market; but nowadays, we simply call up a trucking firm and send the livestock to market in semi trucks.

Still, there is plenty of trailing to be done in the fall, what with moving the cattle around to different pastures and bringing them home to winter ranges. Here again, the working partnership between riders and their horses is most pronounced.

I recall a horse known as "White Cloud" that usually managed to liven up the day for all around. Whenever his rider would lean over to open a gate without dismounting, this unpredictable horse would swiftly jump over the fence.

On one occasion, a bunch of cowboys were looking for a shallow crossing in a fast-moving creek. While they were riding along the bank speculating, White Cloud merely jumped in without warning. He picked the worst possible spot too. It was a deep hole where he entered, but not far across. So, while he spilled his rider on the opposite bank, poor old White Cloud went clear under and came up snorting and pawing at the bank. He scrambled out and shook water all over his rider, who was by then laughing as hard as the others were across the creek.

Dipping cattle in the fall is done to kill the lice that would otherwise live as parasites, weakening the animals during the rigorous wintertime when they need all their strength just to survive. We have a dipping vat on the ranch and in some years, hundreds of cattle are run down the long chute to drop off into it. In this way, many cattle can be dipped in a short time. Afterward, they lie about in the warm fall sunshine looking for all the world as though they enjoyed their strong bath.

Weaning time comes when the calves must be separated from their mothers so the brood cow can build up her bodily reserves for the upcoming calf she will have in the spring. For several days, the cows run around bawling hoarsely, looking for their calves and hanging around the corrals where the calves are bawling back forlornly and looking through fences. In just a few days, however, everything settles down again. The cows go out to graze and stay there while the calves adjust to their new home and feed.

During the winter, the rancher is kept busy feeding all of the hay and grain he worked so hard all summer to put up. The cattle must be fed, come what may, when the snow is deep or when the grass is all grazed off. Then all events must be scheduled around the cattle feeding. Cattle must also have water if they are being fed hay, so that entails either chopping ice from frozen streams or checking stock pumps.

No, the rancher's life is not exactly glamorous. Most of the time, he goes around in faded, ragged clothes, smelling like the barn, and with a sweat-stained hat pulled down over his sun-darkened face. Even on Sundays, which my husband calls a day of rest, it seems he always just takes a little drive out to salt a bunch of cattle, fix a gate, or maybe then fix a tire that he got cactus in while salting the cattle.

A good rancher knows his cattle and, once seeing one, can pick it out of the bunch again. I'm not a good rancher. That's why I was glad when John decided, a few years ago, to number all our cattle on the hip. This way, I can tell them apart (if I can read the numbers), and the calves are also eartagged at birth with a corresponding number.

One big advantage to this system is that, when he leaves, he can tell me to keep an eye on heifers number such and such, which he thinks will calve that day. Or, he might send the kids out and tell them to bring in a cow with a certain number. This way, there is no mix-up. It sure beats the old way when I used to hear things like, "Watch the one that lost her calf in the river last year," or, "Remember that cow that calved by the big tree last year?"

Besides Herefords, we have a few head of dairy stock about the place. These we use for nurse cows to raise any extra calves that are left motherless for some reason. One of these dairy cows is a big Holstein, tall as a man, mean as sin and tough as nails. She used to be a two-man cow. I say this because she wouldn't let anyone go near the barn if anyone strange was around. She wouldn't allow any of our children, which she saw every day, near her, and she quickly pawed up dirt, snorted and put the run on any newcomers about.

One evening, when I was coming home from town, I decided to let the kids take the car on to the house, and I'd get out and walk the quarter mile in with the milk cow. It would save me walking back out to the field to get her. I stepped out of the car. The kids drove away, leaving me to confront a mean cow in my town clothes, which she had never seen before.

She raised her head menacingly and blew her nose. All right, I thought, I'll take off this fancy scarf I'm wearing. I jerked it off and stuffed it down into my jacket pocket. Still she kept me at bay. Okay, I'll go farther, I thought, as I pulled off my back-combed high crown wig with the up-flip and jammed it, also, into my pocket. Now I looked like the real me again, or so I thought. But I hadn't reckoned on the cow not liking my billowing, brightly-colored bell-bottom pants. We rotated in a circle, appraising one another.

Finally my patience wore thin and I bellowed at her.

"I'm not taking off my pants, so you'd better get to the barn, you crazy old fool!" I shouted at her.

That did it. She recognized me then, turned around docilcly and sauntered off homeward. I've often wondered what anyone would have thought if they would have come upon me walking the milk cow home carrying my wig and my pants.

Sometimes I think people tend to forget that all those delicious smelling hamburgers and weiners barbecuing over the glowing coals were once part of a beef. Those thick, tender steaks in candle-lit supper clubs once walked around and were tended by some sunburned, frostbitten, tired rancher.

Endless hours of hard labor, day after day, is the rancher's way of life. He puts meat on America's tables, getting little recognition and, many times, little compensation for it. Still, he wouldn't change places with anyone. You can bet he isn't doing it for the money because, many years, there isn't any money in it. He does it because he likes to be a free man, free to make his own mistakes without government regulations telling him what to do and how to do it.

He likes animals, his fellow man, and he obviously likes nature and the great outdoors. Otherwise, he would be seeking a high-paying job in town with regular hours and vacations. Many ranchers are highly qualified for good positions. Offhand, I can think of two who have degrees in engineering. Yet, they are out there shoveling hay alongside their neighbor, who may not even have a high school diploma.

Besides the labor and wearing elements, there is the very real risk involved in ranching. Two of my good friends were killed outright in tractor accidents, and many more have had disabling injuries. Our own son was hospitalized with a brain concussion incurred in a mishap while chasing horses. Working around horses and cattle is always dangerous. When a stockman is hospitalized for over two months with a broken pelvis, you know it is working a hardship on his family and neighbors in more ways than the usual monetary ones.

As Top Hand so ably sums it up with his droll humor, "We sure as heck ain't in it for the money, and we don't need any more experience!"

Country Wives or Cheap Help

"A time to weep, and a time to laugh. . ."
Ecclesiates 3:4

I was standing deep in thought studying the tobacco display when the store manager came over.

"Could I help you find something?" he asked pleasantly.

"Well, I'm looking for the cheapest tobacco you have," I answered him.

His deft hands sorted through the piles and came up with two brightly colored foil pouches.

"We have this kind and this other one here is mint flavored. Both are in the lower price range," he said as he smilingly proffered the sacks for my inspection.

"Which would you like?" he wanted to know.

"Oh, it doesn't matter," I answered as I took the plain variety and turned away to the check-out counter. "I'm only buying it for my chickens," I threw back as I hurried away.

A few minutes later as I collected my change and prepared

to leave the store with my pre-schooler in tow, I realized the manager was covertly watching me. Then I remembered I hadn't explained, and the poor man probably thought I was off my rocker to buy tobacco for a bunch of hens!

Actually, I used the tobacco to put in the nest to kill the lice and mites which plague the hens. I had many hens setting on eggs and, during the twenty-one days it takes for chicken eggs to hatch, the lice can literally eat the hens alive. A sprinkling of tobacco leaves over the hen and in each nest helps tremendously in combating this problem.

If farm and ranch women tend to be absent-minded at times, I think they have good reason to be. The day I bought the tobacco, I had risen before five in the morning to feed more than forty bum lambs, take care of many different varieties of poultry and came back in the house to make a huge ranch breakfast at six-thirty.

After breakfast, there was the usual hubbub of children leaving for school and a multitude of pets to feed. When the house quieted down after the youngsters' departure, it was time to dress and feed the pre-schooler, do dishes and straighten things up a bit. I was setting a big batch of bread dough when my husband came in and asked me to make a fast trip to town for some veterinary supplies. I dropped everything, grabbed up the youngster and sped to town where I picked up the necessary medication and purchased the tobacco before rushing homeward.

Upon reaching home, I was greeted by bread dough creeping over the sides of the bowl and across the table top, three surveyors I wasn't expecting for dinner and hungry lambs. While I quickly fed the noisy lambs, I concentrated on what I would fix for dinner for four men. I hadn't taken any meat out of the deepfreeze and the refrigerator contained only a few leftovers. Luckily, like most ranch women, I keep some food on hand for just such emergencies, such as frozen meat loaves and casseroles. Then my only problem was how to get everything thawed and bubbly hot by mealtime.

A rancher or farmer must be a mechanic, plumber, electrician, carpenter, veterinarian, weatherman, cowboy, architect, organizer, businessman and boss. But his wife must also be many things. She must be a bookkeeper, a short order cook able to feed any number without advance notice, a nursemaid to sick animals, a gardener, a painter, a driver or an operator of any machine on the place, a chore boy, a minor repairman, a message bearer, and must be able to *follow instructions.*

A country woman must be resourceful and remain calm even though there is a calf in the bathtub, a frozen pump thawing out on the dining room floor and company coming in half an hour.

My mother is a very resourceful person who takes everything in stride. One day her car quit running on a very lonely mountain road and, being very tired, she didn't relish the idea of walking miles for help. Wearily, she opened the hood and stared at the complicated maze of wires and hoses. Then she spied what appeared to be a broken wire. Lacking anything to make repairs with, she calmly removed a bit of elastic string from an undergarment and used it to tie the wires together. The car started immediately and she was able to drive the fifteen miles home without further incident.

During the lean years of wartime, when turkeys paid many of our bills for us, Mom used a bit of ingenuity that I believe deserves recognition. One year, the turkey nests had been hard to find and eggs were in short supply. So, when she discovered a precious turkey egg she resolved to save it, even though it was cracked. She taped it up with a bit of transparent tape and slipped it under a setting hen along with the other eggs. Her determination was rewarded twenty-eight days later when a lusty little turkey emerged from the taped-up speckled egg shell.

This clever woman discovered a way to keep her hens from freezing during a severe cold spell. The hens were housed in a drafty old coop that wasn't insulated. At night, she covered them on the roost with a quilt, and they contentedly survived the cold winter without so much as a frosted comb. Every morning they waited for her to uncover them. She was rewarded by their happy chicken talk and the sight of steam rising from around the corners of the old quilt.

My sister, Fay, is one of the most capable women I know. Not only did she perform all the duties of a ranch wife, but she also taught school for many years, took care of an elderly relative and raised seven fine children. All this was done thirty-five miles from any town, and the handful of neighbors all lived at great distances from her. She was further burdened by having hired men to cook for and by the fact that it was many years before rural telephone and electric lines reached their isolated ranch. Even with their doubtful roads and solitary location, they received much company. She always managed to serve big meals to them with only a few tosses of her coppery hair.

One time this ingenious woman was driving homeward from town with her seven small children in the car. A sudden rainstorm had come up, making the road extremely slippery. She kept going, however, until she high-centered in a rut and there she stopped. It was still miles to home and at least ten miles to any neighbor. She knew it would be a long, long wait until her husband came looking for her. Ranchers are notorious for being absorbed in their work and not missing the cook until at least an hour *after* mealtime. Having a watermelon in the car, she efficiently broke it over the car's bumper, and the youngsters stood around on the damp grass in the barrow pit enjoying a picnic which helped lighten the moods of everyone during the long delay.

Another sister, Flora, keeps up a beautiful acre of lawn, flowers, shubbery and fruit trees. Besides the usual woes of gardeners, she has the added worry of rattlesnakes. They curl up in her shady flower beds on hot days and, on cool days, they stretch their perilous lengths across her cement patio for warmth. She frequently meets them in her strawberry bed or sees them enjoying the cooling effects of the lawn sprinkler. One summer, after many close calls with their poisonous fangs, she resorted to wearing heavy hot rubber overshoes every week while pushing the lawnmower over her lawn.

A ranch wife must be a fearless soul. Joan, another of my sisters, is a good example. One dark night after company left, she went to her chicken house to gather the eggs in pitch darkness. She thrust her hand unhesistantly into each nest and soon had her apron filled with eggs. A couple of the nests had broody hens setting on them, so she wasn't too alarmed when she shoved her hand into the last nest and encountered a warm body. But she froze as her fingers touched a wet broken egg, thick fur, and a pointed nose! It was a skunk eating eggs. Luckily for her, the skunk was as surprised as she was and he neglected to use his most effective weapon on her.

This same gal got up every half hour for several nights to check her orchard by flashlight until she discovered a porcupine, the culprit, that was eating her young trees. Another time, she helped her husband chase down and tree a Canadian lynx through a vast undergrowth of willows and rosebushes, although she was protected by nothing more than a light dress, slippers and her unquenchable spirit.

A country wife has many dilemmas to face, aside from her regular work. Quite often she is obliged to put up "strays" for the night. These strays might be truckers, lost hunters, storm-trapped travelers, salesmen or hubby's dear army buddies not heard from in twenty years until they show up with at least six kids each.

On top of this, she probably has a finicky hired man who sits down to a good meal with the comment, "This wouldn't be too bad if you only added a little spice."

A ranch wife goes hopefully on, even after the mice have chewed off her blossoming tomato plants, the toddler has eaten her celery plants for the third time, and she has awakened to find that thirty head of yearlings have gotten into the garden overnight.

A ranch woman's life can also be hazardous. She can easily fall from a hayloft or from a scaffold while painting the high barn. She is subject to black eyes and bumps on the head while helping put cattle through a stubborn metal chute. She knows the milk cow kicks viciously and yet, undaunted, she goes out to milk anyway. The day the mailman tells her there are forty head of yearlings in the new alfalfa, she boldly saddles the only horse in the corral and he happens to be a snaky unpredictable animal.

She doctors all the animals on the place and yet staggers around herself with walking pneumonia in the wet spring, mumbling, "I'm okay – just a touch of flu." Never can she relax with always so much to do. A mountain of overalls waits to be mended, the eggs piling up need washing, company is coming for supper, but first she must make a fast trip to town to pick up a part for the plow.

Even though it's Parents' Night at the high school and she's had her hair done at the beauty shop, the ranch wife pulls on a parka and goes out in twenty mile an hour winds and snow to help feed the calves. Later that night, sitting in the back row on stage of the high school auditorium, she slips her shoe unobtrusively from her swollen foot. A yearling bull happened to kick at her when she was pouring out their grain. Maybe, if they aren't vaccinating cattle the next day, she can get in to a doctor for X-rays.

A ranch wife must share her home with all manner of living things. Once, during a late spring snowstorm, many of our honey bees, which live only thirty feet from our kitchen door, flew into the soft snowdrifts and were firmly embedded. Our daughter, Marion, conscientiously picked them out, one by one, and brought them into the house to warm up. When they began crawling over her hands and arms, she put them into jars with a bit of honey in each one for food. She kept a close watch on the area around the hive, repeatedly coming in with handfuls of the chilled bees.

A couple of days later, when the weather warmed, she released them outside to go on about their business. I can't say that I objected, but I did get a bit nervous whenever she opened the jars in the kitchen and let the bees crawl over her hands. I could visualize the house swarming with them.

One cold winter Sunday afternoon my sister decided to go into her unheated root cellar for potatoes and canned fruit. Her helpful husband filled two pails with hot ashes from their coal furnace to offset the warmth lost by opening the doors. No sooner had they entered the cellar when the dogs set up an uproar. Her husband went out to investigate, leaving her to get the supplies. But, without thinking, he hooked both cellar doors behind him.

In the yard, he found a neighbor had come visiting so they talked a few minutes before moving into the house. There he called for his wife to make coffee, but discovered she wasn't around. He shouted loudly both upstairs and down and his outbursts woke the baby, whose cries added to the confusion.

Finally the husband picked up the squalling infant and sat down to resume his visit with the neighbor but still puzzled by his wife's absence.

Meanwhile, back in the cellar, my sister was fuming at being inadvertently locked in. After nearly an hour in the chilly damp darkness, her anger and desperation drove her to such superhuman strength that she broke both doors open and escaped.

When my sister angrily entered her kitchen with cobwebs in her hair and smelling like a musty cellar, her husband guiltily remembered where she'd been. The consequence of that episode was that, in wrecking the cellar doors, their entire stock of potatoes froze.

The epitome of a ranch wife's life is best told by what happened to my sister on one occasion when she was helping her husband. Driving a heavy truckload of feed, she buried it down to the axles in a grass-concealed boghole her husband had neglected to warn her about.

He turned his own loaded truck around and went back to the ranch buildings for a Caterpillar with which to pull his spouse out. Some time later, when he returned with the Caterpillar, his weepy wife confronted him with, "Aren't you even going to get mad and holler?"

With a resigned shrug, he answered her, "What else can you expect from such cheap help?"

12

Living the Good Life

"Lord, our Lord, how glorious is your name over all the earth!"
Psalm 8:10

The time is one-thirty in the morning and the cool, silver moonlight floods the landscape with its beautiful magic enchantment. I am listening to the hiss of the pressure cooker as I process the last of the front quarter of beef I'm canning.

Canning beef is a tiresome task at any time; but, with youngsters underfoot, I always feel it is best done at night when they are safely tucked into bed. And the canned meat will be a lifesaver during the busy days of spring ahead.

The house is very still and peaceful, except for the sound of the pressure cooker; a thousand memories come to mind as I sit waiting for the meat to be done.

My earliest recollections go back to a one-room schoolhouse called Ripley School, up on the prairies about twenty miles from the Canadian border.

Once again, I'm sitting on the schoolhouse step on a soft, warm, spring evening, watching the violet dusk descend while I blow soap bubbles with an old wooden spool and a bar of soap. This was a treat reserved only for when I was very good, as soap was precious.

It was wartime and, like nearly everyone else, we were very hard up, only I didn't realize it at the time. Mom was most fortunate in securing this teaching position in such a fine community. But, when we moved into the schoolhouse, it was two months before we got into town again. During that time, we didn't even have kerosene to light the dark evenings. With a rag in a dish of grease, my resourceful mother improvised a poor substitute for a lamp, which had to suffice.

Though we had enough to eat, we would now probably turn up our noses at what then seemed like fine food. When the apples froze in the cupboard, we simply ate them anyway. Mom cooked on the potbellied heating stove, and I thought we lived very well. Lacking an iron, she scoured off the bottom of the heavy frying pan in the ash pile, heated it on the stove and ironed our clothes with it until we looked presentable. Our hair was curled by rolling it up on rags. The rags certainly were more comfortable to sleep on than the modern day hair rollers, but created a slightly frizzy look.

We saw large herds of antelope containing several hundred head, looking like bands of sheep, roving over the prairies past the little schoolhouse in their restless search for food and safety.

Often, horse-drawn wagonloads of Indians passed by on their slow way to another reservation. These wagons were filled with Indians and heaped high with their belongings. There was always the added fascination of several colorful riders in the caravan, and many dogs. During the time they were passing, I remained very still, which was hard for me to do, but I was afraid of being "given to the Indians," as I'd been threatened with. No one else ever passed by, so it was a thrilling spectacle.

The neighborhood was most congenial and we were invited to different homes to eat, which was a great treat. One Norwegian family by the name of Halingstad lived on North Fork Creek and became long, fast friends of ours.

I vividly recollect the time Gudrun Halingstad sent a cup of cream over to the schoolhouse, and Mom promised me that if I behaved well, she would mix up a chocolate cake when school let out. This cake batter would then be poured into the old frying pan and set upon dying coals in the heating stove until a broom straw showed it was done. It would be delicious.

So, I was a good girl and sat quietly throughout the long afternoon in the schoolroom while she taught. But I stirred the cup of cream while I waited. At last, school was dismissed and the children went to catch their horses, saddle up and ride home. I was very excited over the prospect of chocolate cake; then absolutely unconsolable when Mom took up the cup of cream and announced happily that it had begun to turn into butter.

We seldom had butter, so Mom and my sister thought it was a great treat to have bread with fresh butter. Not me! I cried great salty tears and, though I was only three years old, I've never forgotten the time we had bread and butter instead of chocolate cake.

The Halingstads had two boys, one of whom was only slightly older than I. His name was Eldon. We were both too young to attend classes, so we alternately fought and played peacefully.

Once, while the school children and Mom were busily engaged in a fast game of "Annie-I-Over" the schoolhouse with the ball, Eldon and I amused ourselves by playing in the ash pile and flinging ashes around. We were having a fine time until a large piece of ash embedded itself in my eye and I went dashing off to tattle to Mom.

With great composure, she told me crying was good, and then dispatched one of the older boys to fetch a piece of horsehair. This coarse bit of hair she folded into a loop and, with some careful maneuvering, was able to remove the offending ash from my eye. I was cautioned against throwing ashes and sent back again to play.

These were hard and trying times for the grown-ups, but we children led a blissfully contented life. We made up games, dug in the dirt, splashed in the creek, jumped from the tops of old buildings, romped in the hay, chased each other around outside in the dark and, in general, had a splendid time. We were oblivious to the grim news and the dark clouds of war.

I'm sure the students at Ripley School must have invented several novel games. Lacking playground equipment and entertaining material, they made their own. "Streaking" was invented there, long before it became a national sport thirty years later. The oldest grade school girl took off her clothes one evening and ran around the outside of the schoolhouse, but no one was present except for my mother, sister and me. Another time, she removed her shoes and stockings and ran outside into the snow.

Since all the youngsters rode horseback to school at that time, the school yard was literally "littered." One important pastime was grading the horse manure. I can remember the piled heaps of the most perfect whole pieces, labeled grade "A", and other piles varying in context and grade.

Many folks will be shocked to read this, but it was a most

serious amusement to those prairie children playing without the benefit of recreation equipment such as our children enjoy today.

The youngsters also undertook to make a mock grave in a shallow coulee nearby for the last teacher they had had who had been extremely mean to them all.

Gradually, the years slipped away with more wars and rumors of wars. We lived in an up-and-down economic situation governed by the rise and fall of livestock prices. Nothing was ever secure, but we always anticipated something; and there was a strong feeling of achievement in all we did or accomplished.

Even milking an ornery old milk cow out in the corral during a bleak grey evening, with the tranquil flakes of snow sifting down and dripping wetly into your coat collar, isn't so bad. Not when you can look forward to next year when the barn will be finished and you'll have a nice warm place to milk and do chores in.

When you're raking hay and trying to keep an eagle-eye on the children playing among the willows along the edge of the field, you can look forward to next year when your husband will buy a hay swather so you can stay out of the hayfield and do your own work.

Although you're two miles from home with a small baby, helping your husband sew up a prolapsed cow during a fierce blizzard, there is something to look forward to. You console yourself with the thought that next year, the baby will be older and easier to take along on these vital ranch duties.

Even a tired mind can dream ahead unrestrained while your hands are busy treating sick lambs and calves. When the baby chicks arrive during a late spring snowstorm and the power goes off, leaving the brooder a cold, useless hulk, the chicks must be taken into the house for warmth. But still you're sure it won't happen again, and you order early again the next year.

The pressure cooker continues its hissing as I visualize our family of stalwart youths and find hope for the morrow. The jovial, infectious energy of the young is an excellent antidote for a chaotic world.

A lump rises in my throat when I think of our oldest son, Elgin, and remember the lonely vigils at his bedside when we didn't know if he'd ever see the sun rise again. Now, the husky lad gallops his horse across the fields and is a far cry from the puny boy who struggled so long just to live. Every year, he grew in health until the battle was won. It was no small victory.

Our second, and youngest, son is the "special" boy in the family. We adopted Luke when he was only three weeks old; and his intelligence, good humor and bright little face has added a new dimension to all our lives. The uncluttered world of a four-year-old is so beautifully simple that it's a pleasure to try once again to see it through his eyes. Of course, our mainstay is the girls. With their unswerving, cheerful loyalty, Marion and Jody have truly illuminated this world for us.

Trying to build up a ranch from "scratch" is a stupendous effort requiring the aid of the whole family. Many were the times that we lived on little more than hope; but we kept going onward to "next year" with a strong sense of destiny. A host of warm friends and relatives lent their strength to flagging spirits, and added encouragement when the chips were down. I believe that experiencing hard times and trouble creates a greater bond between people than they would otherwise have. I feel a closeness toward my three sisters, Joan, Fay and Flora, that I might not have, had we been brought up with everything and gone our different ways separately.

Recollections wing their way into my mind. Recollections of good time shared with friends, as well as times of deep sorrow and grieving. I sadly recall the face of a beloved family member who was taken swiftly from us in a grinding auto crash. I remember another dear friend who fought a valiant fight against cancer, never letting anything show except her indomitable good spirits, until at last the malignant monster was victorious.

I look back with nostalgia to childhood days in the cool spring when I went boating in the shallow streams with an old washtub. Even the chilly wetness could not quench the lively flame of youthful optimism. By the way, a washtub makes a lousy boat.

I still recoil when remembering the time I fearfully hid in the woodshed to avoid some disreputable hired men. The men had been paid off and left. Then everyone else on the ranch departed for town also, leaving me home all alone. My folks had only just gone when the car full of itinerant hay hands returned. In fright, I fled the house and hid in the woodshed out in the back yard. I watched through a crack in the wall as they entered the house and searched the shop for things to steal. They didn't know anyone was at home, and they apparently didn't think the nondescript woodshed was worth looking into. I was weak with relief when they at last piled into their sagging car and left.

With a smile now, I can recall the time my mother broke some ribs while working in the lambing shed. She bound herself up with dish towels and continued her work, never telling anyone until several weeks later when the breaks were nearly healed up. About all she would say then was that it sure had hurt to cough!

I remember with pleasure the excitement and joy of a new baby in the house. The watery smile of an infant with all its tiny physical perfections mirrors the greatness of God's design for the universe.

The magic of a spring sunset or a rainbow, a vibrant green field dotted with lazily grazing cattle with fresh white-faced calves, and the pearly mornings when frost clings to every object, giving pristine quality to the world, are all priceless experiences. The quick thundershower that rolls away, leaving sunshine in its wake, and the clean smell of warm, moist earth awakens a drab soul and revitalizes the spirit. Even though the rancher lives and works with the forces of nature, he never ceases to be amazed and awed by them. There is a promise in each new day that dawns.

We ranchers are all living out here in "next year country" and we aren't likely to leave it. Despite everything, it is still a pretty good place to be.